New England Rails

1948 - 1968

by David R. Sweetland

all photography by the author except as noted

Copyright © 1989
Morning Sun Books, Inc.

Published by
Morning Sun Books, Inc.
11 Sussex Court
Edison, N.J. 08820
Library of Congress Catalog Card Number: 89-90846
Layout and typesetting by R.J. Yanosey, Morning Sun Books, Inc.

First Printing
ISBN # 0-9619058-4-0

This book is dedicated to my late father, William H. Sweetland, an early New England rail photographer.

Acknowledgements

For all the railroaders and fans who liked the New England rail scene, this book and color photography is for you.

My wife helped with the initial writing stages for this book and years ago sat patiently in the car knitting while I was waiting for a train. Sue, a native of Maine and a fellow graduate of the University of Maine, led me to all those remote Maine railroad junctions to record the action on Kodachrome. This complimented my southern New England photography from my parents' home in Providence, R.I. Our oldest son Ross supplied all the sketches of the railroad junctions with his architectural background from RI School of Design. Our other children, Christopher, Elizabeth and Joyann also helped in the preparation of this book, making it a total family project.

Slides from four other excellent color photographers, Mike Bullock, Ralph Phillips, Mike Usenia and Bob Watson were used to help in sections of this six state area. Bill Clynes and Ben Perry helped by furnishing technical information about the New Haven. After the initial writing, Frank Tatnall spent many hours of editing to enhance the script. The NHRHTA reviewed the New Haven part of this book. Back in 1984, Don Ball talked to me about using some of my PRR photography for his book and this got me interested in putting together a book. But it was Bob Yanosey who gave me the opportunity to publish my material. Without his help, the project never would have been accomplished.

Introduction

The railroads of New England have always been interesting because of the great diversity of ownership of rail lines in a small territory and the diversity of equipment. This book will show the variety of motive power utilized for train operations during the fifties from the high density electrified territory of the New Haven to the backwoods branchlines of Maine. No two lines were the same or were operated in the same manner. Covered are the transition years from steam and electric locomotives to first generation diesels. A brief look at the diesel locomotive purchases leads us into the colorful times of the *New England Rails*.

The diesel era for the New England railroads really started back in 1931 with the delivery of high hood #0900 to the New Haven. The unit was the prototype for Alco's production of switching locomotives during the 1930's and the forerunner for the dieselization of all yard switching operations in the 1940's. B&M purchased the 1934 high hood demonstrator #602 and renumbered it #1102, later #1160. Dieselization of passenger operations came with the FLYING YANKEE, a Budd built articulated train with a Winton model 201-A diesel engine. This 1935 train seated 142 in three cars for the B&M/MEC on the Boston to Bangor run.

In 1934, the B&M took delivery of one 600hp twin engine center-cab switcher. The GE unit with Ingersoll-Rand diesel engines had the same machinery as in the GE box cab units. The next interesting development for diesel switchers was an order by the New Haven for ten special GE units built at Erie, Pa. These "oil electric" locomotives with interchangeable diesel engines, five with Ingersoll-Rand and

five with Cooper Bessemer diesel engines, had common car bodies, radiators, trucks and electrical equipment. Although they looked like small road switchers, the radiator compartment was actually in the short hood. Delivered to the New Haven as #0901 to #0910 in 1936, they worked the New Haven, Conn. area until 1953 when five were sold to the BAR. #0906 to #0909 were later scrapped and #0910 sold to the Atlantic Coal Co. in Maine. The BAR purchased the #0901 to #0905 group with Cooper Bessemer diesel engines and renumbered them #30 to #34. While on the BAR, they started out in New Haven green, some were later repainted blue and gray, and at least two of them became dark blue. With a double reduction gear, their top speed was limited to 25 mph, but they could pull anything in the yard. The last of the units was finally retired in 1967 and traded in on new GP38's for the BAR.

A fleet of aging steam locomotives forced the New Haven to consider purchasing new power. Ten streamlined 4-6-4's had been built by Baldwin in 1937 and were added to the fleet, but it was obvious that more were needed to cover all the mainline passenger assignments. The New Haven then turned back to its long time friend Alco for help. Alco had been working with the Rock Island to develop and produce a 2000hp twin engine passenger unit. In 1941, the New Haven received delivery of ten DL109's, #0700 to #0709, just in time for the increasing traffic levels along the Shore Line route. After some modifications to the roof vents and cooling systems, New Haven ran the wheels off these units in both freight and passenger service making two and one half round trips a day between New Haven and Boston. The dual service units were so successful that the New Haven was able to convince the War Production Board to allow Alco to produce more units, so that a total of sixty DL109's were running on the New Haven by April of 1945.

The B&M started diesel freight service with the delivery of forty eight FT's in 1943 and 1944. Back in September 1940, the EMD FT demonstrator had convinced the B&M that FT's could handle road freights. EMD #103 demonstrator set handled 6,500 tons of freight from East Deerfield to Mechanicville without electrics in Hoosac Tunnel, a 48% increase in tonnage over the newest 4-8-2's. In 1946, the B&M received fifteen single F2 A units in order to split some of the four unit FT sets in half. An FT A&B would be matched up with an F2A to form a three unit A-B-A combination. In addition, the B&M received three A-B sets, #4224 A&B to 4226 A&B, with steam generators for passenger service. The F2 was the predecessor to the more famous 1500hp F3, having the same carbody but rated at only 1350hp.

(Robert Watson photo)

1947 was the turning point for diesel road units in New England with a large increase in diesel production. After extensive testing with the FA demonstrators in 1946, the New Haven ordered 15 A-B-A sets of FA's to cover the Maybrook Line. Starting delivery in May of 1947, the 45 FA's would push 43 New Haven 2-10-2's into retirement.

Up in Maine, the Maine Central obtained a four unit set of F3's with the two B units having steam generators for passenger operation. In October 1947, the BAR started dieselization when EMD delivered two A-B-A sets of F3's. The following year, the BAR would receive two more A-B-A sets of F3's. However, this time the last two A units were equipped with steam generators for passenger service. Several years later, these B units would be sold to the PRR.

Even the Boston and Albany got into the act, when the New York Central diesel road power started to run over the B&A. FA1's #1000 to #1003 and FB1's #2300 and #2301 were assigned to the B&A. F3's #1606-#1623 along with the B units were frequent visitors to the B&A in 1947. By 1948, the 5000 series New York Central 2000hp Erie builts joined more FA's to handle most of the road tonnage on the B&A. A black and white photograph exists of a A-B-B-A set of Erie builts on the B&A, making it the most powerful locomotive consist in New England at that time.

Maine Central added six more F3A units to its roster and the Boston & Maine added two F3A's and two F3B's. Since these units were delivered very late in F3 production and equipped with F7 side grills, they were often referred to as F5's.

It was the RS2 that made a major impact on the locomotive market in New England. In October of 1946, Alco introduced the RS2 as a higher horsepower road switcher. The RS2 era in New England started at the end of 1947 with the delivery of ten to the New Haven. These dual equipped units, #0500 to #0509, covered both passenger and freight runs on the Danbury, Conn. to Pittsfield, Mass. line. In May 1948, the B&M purchased ex Alco RS2 demonstrator #1500 to test on their railroad. Keeping the #1500, which was delivered in switcher colors, the B&M was sold on the road switcher concept. Two months later, the B&M received the first of four BL2's, branchline units #1550-#1553. During 1948, the Southern Railway cancelled a four unit order for BL2's and the B&M stepped in to pick up the units. Delivered in July and September, these BL2's were received with steam generators, but without MU. They were used for Boston commuter service and local operations around White River Jct.

The New Haven continued its road switcher purchases with seven more RS2's in 1948. In March the New Haven added their first low horsepower road switchers, ten Alco RS1's. Two more 1000hp units were added for local service in November. Another RS1, #8100, was delivered in February to the New York Central for passenger service on the B&A at Boston. Four of the eight NYC freight RS1's, also delivered in 1948, were assigned to B&A locals. Also shipped from Alco in February 1948, were two NYC RS2's, #8200 and #8201. Being the first 1500hp or larger road switchers on the NYC, these two class DRSP-1a's were tried out in commuter passenger service at Boston.

Purchases for road switchers increased in 1949, especially for the Alco RS2's. Following the success of #1500, the Boston & Maine received nine more RS2's. #1501 to #1509 were delivered in March without steam generators for freight service, while #1530 to #1534 were delivered with generators for passenger operation in March and June 1949. Several years later in November 1953, steam generators were added to #1501 to #1504 so they could be used in commuter service. Maine Central joined the RS2 owners' list in January and February, when #551 to #555 started operating in freight service out of Bangor, Maine. For the Vermont operation of the Canadian Pacific, five RS2's were delivered from Alco. These RS2's followed the successful demonstration of Alco RS2 #1501 between Wells River and Montreal in April and May of 1947. The BAR placed the only 1949 EMD road switcher order in New England, BL2's #550-#557. Later renumbered #50-#57, these branchline units lasted into the 1980's.

In 1949 Alco delivered to the CP eight FA1's and four FB1's to dieselize its Newport, Vt. to White River Jct. joint operations. The New York Central had forty-four FA1's and twenty-two FB1's operating on the system, many covering the mountainous territory of the B&A. The Alco FA1 became a more common sight on *New England Rails* than the more popular, nationwide, EMD F7. FA's handled freight assignments on the New Haven, Boston and Albany, and Canadian Pacific. These were joined in the early fifties with eight FA1's from the Canadian National, handling through freights on the Central Vermont.

After three years of production, Fairbanks-Morse had produced thirty-five 1500hp model H-15-44 road switchers. With the classic sloping Loewy lines, curved windows, and rounded headlight mounting, the horsepower was increased to 1600hp by July 1950 to compete with the Alco RS3 and Baldwin AS16.

(Robert Watson photo)

Seven of the new model H-16-44's had been delivered when the New Haven received #560 to #569 in November and December of 1950. This was New Haven's first order of opposed piston diesel power. Equipped with AAR type B road trucks and steam generators, these units were mainly assigned to Providence for operation and maintenance. When the RS3 fleet was expanded, these first units were renumbered #590 to #599.

Lima Hamilton finally entered the diesel locomotive market in 1949 with a line of 750hp and 1000hp switchers. Lima was anxious to obtain new orders to build a base for its production line. In April 1950, the horsepower was raised from 1000hp to 1200hp for the eight cylinder Hamilton diesel engine. New Haven ordered ten 1200hp units with MU for the dieselization of Maybrook yard. Delivered in October through December, the units were used in pairs on the Maybrook hump. Numbered #630 to #639 following the S2's that ended at #621, they were Lima's only New England sale and lasted only about 10 years on the New Haven before being removed from the roster.

In order to capture this exciting time in New England, some of the motive power was recorded on 35mm color film. These colorful locomotives are being rolled out again for us to take a second look. This photographic journey starts at New Rochelle, New York going north through the Connecticut River Valley to the Canadian border, and then along the New England coastline from Connecticut to northern Maine, all in full color from 1948 to 1968.

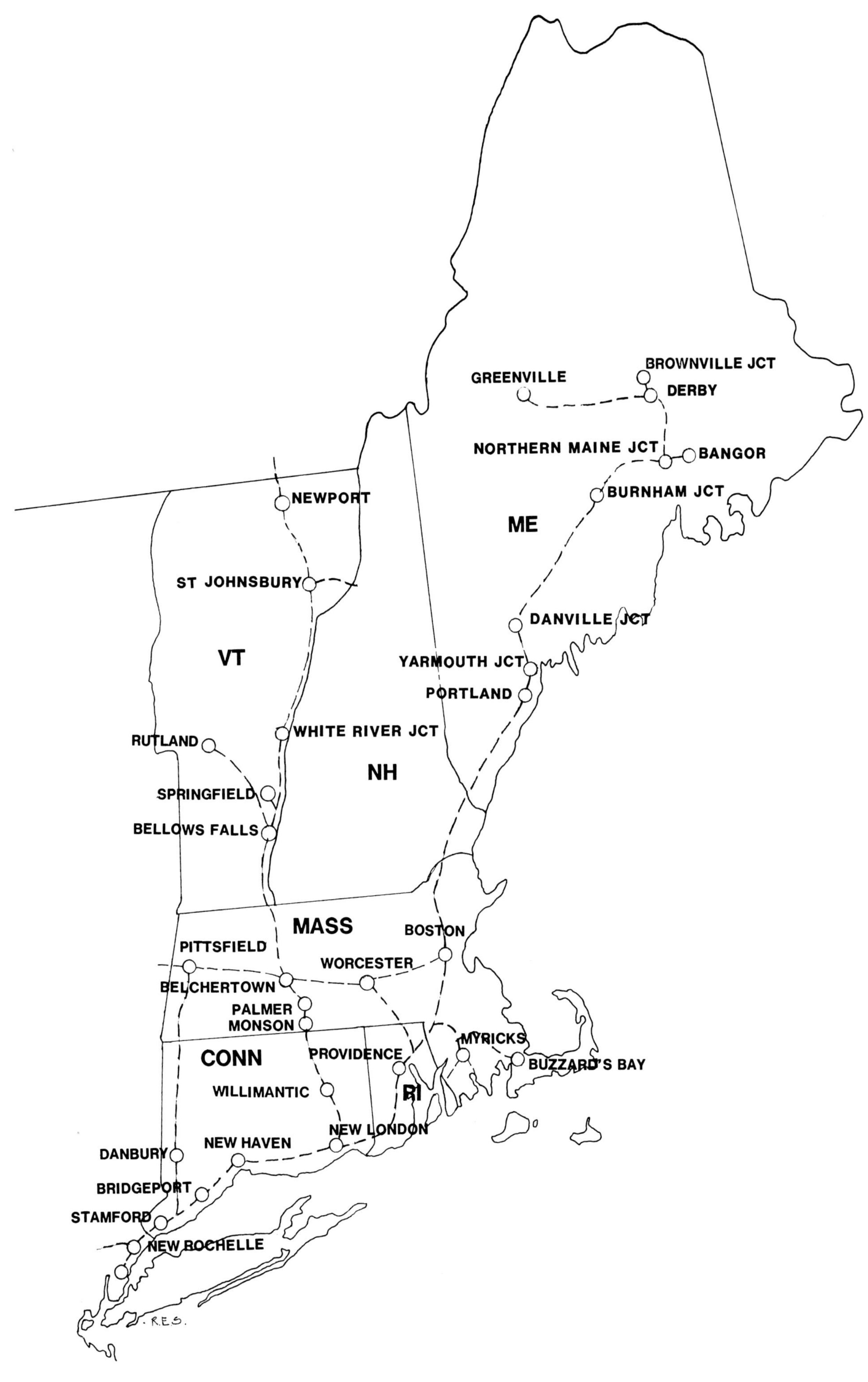

GREENVILLE
BROWNVILLE JCT
DERBY
NORTHERN MAINE JCT
BANGOR
BURNHAM JCT
NEWPORT
ME
ST JOHNSBURY
DANVILLE JCT
VT
YARMOUTH JCT
PORTLAND
RUTLAND
WHITE RIVER JCT
NH
SPRINGFIELD
BELLOWS FALLS
MASS
BOSTON
PITTSFIELD
WORCESTER
BELCHERTOWN
PALMER
MONSON
MYRICKS
CONN
PROVIDENCE
BUZZARD'S BAY
WILLIMANTIC
RI
DANBURY
NEW HAVEN
NEW LONDON
BRIDGEPORT
STAMFORD
NEW ROCHELLE
R.E.S.

New Rochelle, N.Y.

As we turn our clocks back to the fifties, we begin our journey north through New England. The entire rail system at that time was quite different from what it is now, with more variety of colorful equipment and greater emphasis on identification of ownership. Each owner had his own idea on how to run a railroad. The New England railroads had color and understated class, that old yankee flavor. For a small concentrated area, these lines crisscrossed each other often with many junctions. These were the focal point of our color photography excursion to the six state area. Some were controlled by vintage high balls while others by cold steel diamonds. All added to the early railroad charm in the area. At New Rochelle, N.Y., the New Haven's line from Penn Station, New York joined the mainline from Grand Central Terminal: a two track main joining a four track main at SS22 interlocking. Beginning in 1917, through passenger service was started to Penn Station with the opening of Hell Gate Bridge.

(Above) Following the morning rush hour, #81, the oldest EF-1 on the roster, received an air test on the three car local before heading north. After the air had recharged in the brake pipe and an "OK" was received from the car inspector, the local headed north to New England. The date was April 5, 1956.

(Right) A 150 class freight motor passed by with a freight for the car floats at Oak Point and the Long Island connection. Ten of these motors were built during the peak traffic period of WWII, five by GE and five by Baldwin-Westinghouse. In 1956 they ranked as the most powerful locomotives in New England.

Still in the yard awaiting a later run was EY-2b #219 *(above)*. These sturdy steeple cab motors were built for switching the major yards in the electrified zone of the New Haven. This EY-2, built by Baldwin-Westinghouse in August 1926, was retired by the next year in October of 1957. Even with 63" drivers, these motors could not make time on the road locals as they were only geared for 25 mph operation.

New Haven's class EY-2 80 ton steeple cab switch engines from Baldwin-Westinghouse were built in two groups, #0200 to #0214 in 1911 and #0218 to #0223 in 1926. Most of the second group lasted thirty one years in yard service in the electrified zone. In 1944, ex New York, Westchester and Boston #701 was added to the New Haven's roster as #0224. It was almost identical to the first group of EY-2's and was constructed at the same time in 1911.

(Below) A combination baggage and mail trailer led an MU set through New Rochelle on its way to Stamford, doing the mail work for the small commuter stops along the way, its thirty foot mail section loaded with letters for such towns as Cos Cob, Harrison, Rye and Greenwich. Three of these 1915 Bradley Car Corporation MU's lasted into the new MU car era of the New Haven.

Stamford, Conn.

We started our trip to New England by leaving New York State and heading north. Just after crossing into the State of Connecticut, we entered the City of Stamford, population 73,500 in 1950. In 1908, the New Haven completed twenty miles of electrification from Woodlawn, N.Y. to Stamford, Conn. EP-1 passenger electric locomotives ran on  the New York Central 600 volt DC third rail to Woodlawn Jct., and then 11,000 volt AC overhead wire on the New Haven trackage to Stamford. After 1913, through trains changed to steam power at New Haven for the remainder of the trip to Boston or Springfield. In 1899, the first part of the New Haven was electrified, the New Canaan Branch. 8.3 miles long, the branch met the mainline at Stamford. The original electrification was replaced with an AC catenary system when the mainline was electrified in 1908.

(Above) The date was April 1, 1955 and the 370 class electrics were being delivered from GE. After a station stop, #371 handled a train for Grand Central Terminal just after being delivered.

(Below) The newest motor was followed by the oldest freight motors, two EF-1's #109 and #111 built by Baldwin-Westinghouse in 1913, on their way to Oak Point. After two more years of service, these EF-1's were retired following the delivery of the FL-9's. The EF-1 group of freight motors was built during the period 1910 to 1913 and numbered #070 to #0111. The "0" stood for "other than steam." In 1949, thirty of these motors were still in service.

(Above) One year later in April 1956, EP-3 #356 dashed through Stamford on its way to Penn Station, New York. All ten EP-3's were still very active on the roster handling heavy through passenger trains. The first car was one of New Haven's office cars deadheading to the south end of the system. Behind the baggage car was a string of Pullman Standard coaches already painted with the red orange window stripe.

(Below) On the same day, just south of Stamford, an EP-2 rounded a curve on the way to Grand Central powering a train from Boston. #312 was one of the two EP-2's painted in the McGinnis paint scheme. The afternoon scene captured the full effect of the triangular catenary structure and the strikingly clean box motor. From the box cab, the engineer had a picture window view of the tracks ahead.

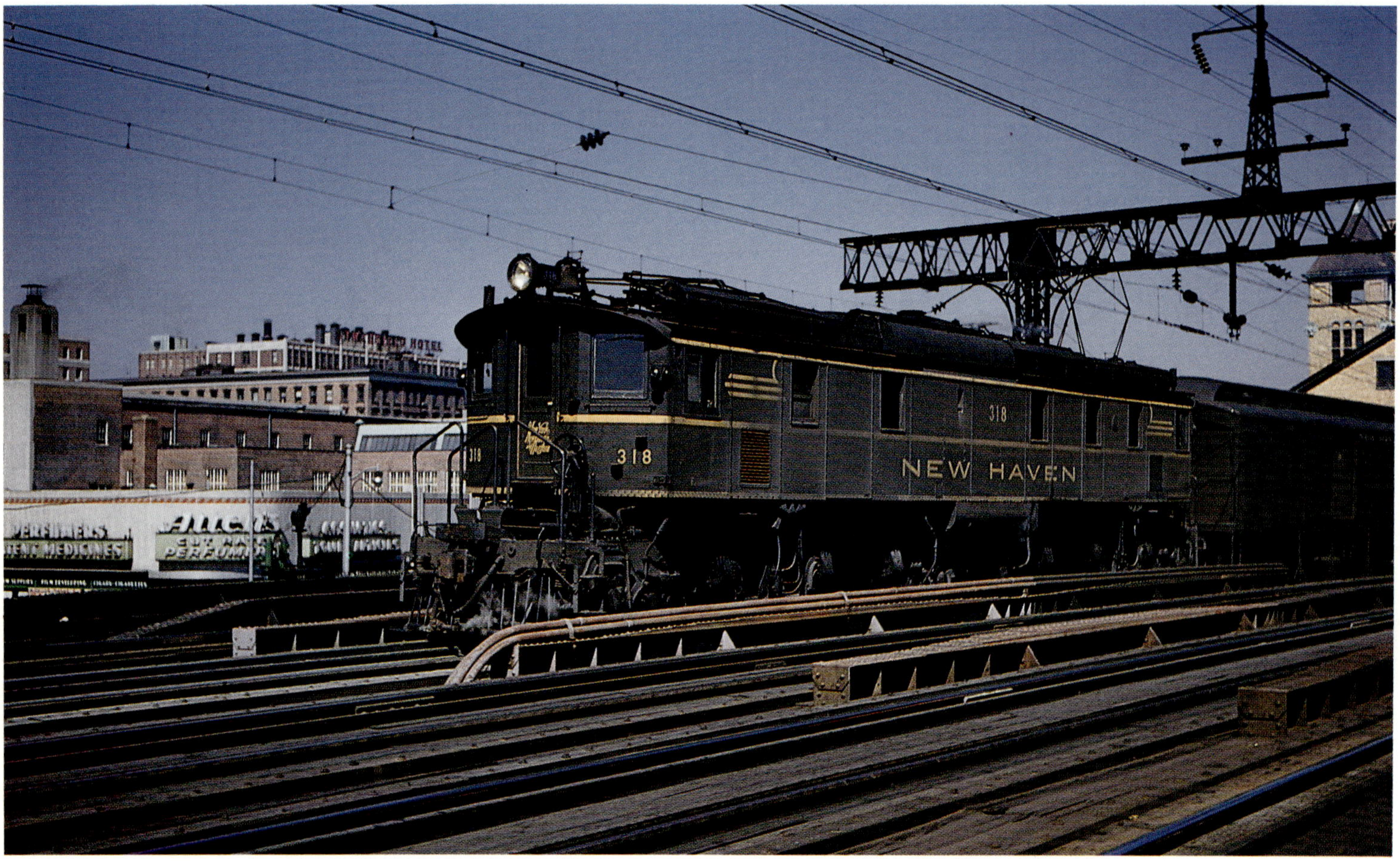

Bridgeport, Conn.

At Bridgeport, EP-2 #318 *(above)* stopped to discharge passengers and mail. Twenty-seven EP-2's were built by Baldwin-Westinghouse between 1918 and 1927. Remaining on the roster until 1958, the 68 foot long EP-2 motors would operate on both 11,000 volt AC or 600 volt DC for the New York Central third rail operation into Grand Central Terminal. It was still cold on that April 1, 1955 and the fireman went back to the middle of the carbody to check on the steam heating boiler during the station stop.

(Opposite page, top) Under the wire on their way to Devon Jct., #0421 led a four unit set of FA's on a Maybrook freight. The two FA-1 "A" units had been repainted in the McGinnis colors. Delivered as five A-B-A sets in 1947, five more "B" units were added in 1951 to make four unit sets as tonnage increased on this line. That second unit was one of the added FB-2's still in its original paint. In just one order, the FA's bumped the 2-10-2's into retirement and dieselized the Maybrook Line.

(Opposite page, bottom) A two year old EP-5 is shown handling five coaches for Boston. New Haven wanted to continue electrification, but #371 never made it to Boston under the wire. No one at that time could have forseen that several EP-5's would wind up in Penn Central black, handling freight trains on the old PRR side. They were no slouch at 87,000 pounds of tractive effort.

Danbury, Conn.

Danbury, Connecticut was the location where the Norwalk, Connecticut to Pittsfield, Massachusetts line crossed the western freight artery of the New Haven, the Maybrook Line. On September 12, 1957, action at the junction started with RS3 #553 *(above)* bringing in the southbound train #141 from Pittsfield, Massachusetts. The line south of Danbury was electrified and a change of power *(opposite page, top)* was required. One hundred and eighty ton EP-2 #322 made the trip. The Baldwin-Westinghouse motor was in the McGinnis paint scheme, one of a few box cabs to have such a distinction. Within two years #322 and the rest of the EP-2's would be retired. *(Opposite page, bottom)* A few hours later, sister motor #311 arrived out of New York City with the northbound train #140 to Pittsfield. #311 stopped at the north-east end of the station on one of the electrified tracks. The two non-electrified tracks to the right were the freight tracks to Maybrook.

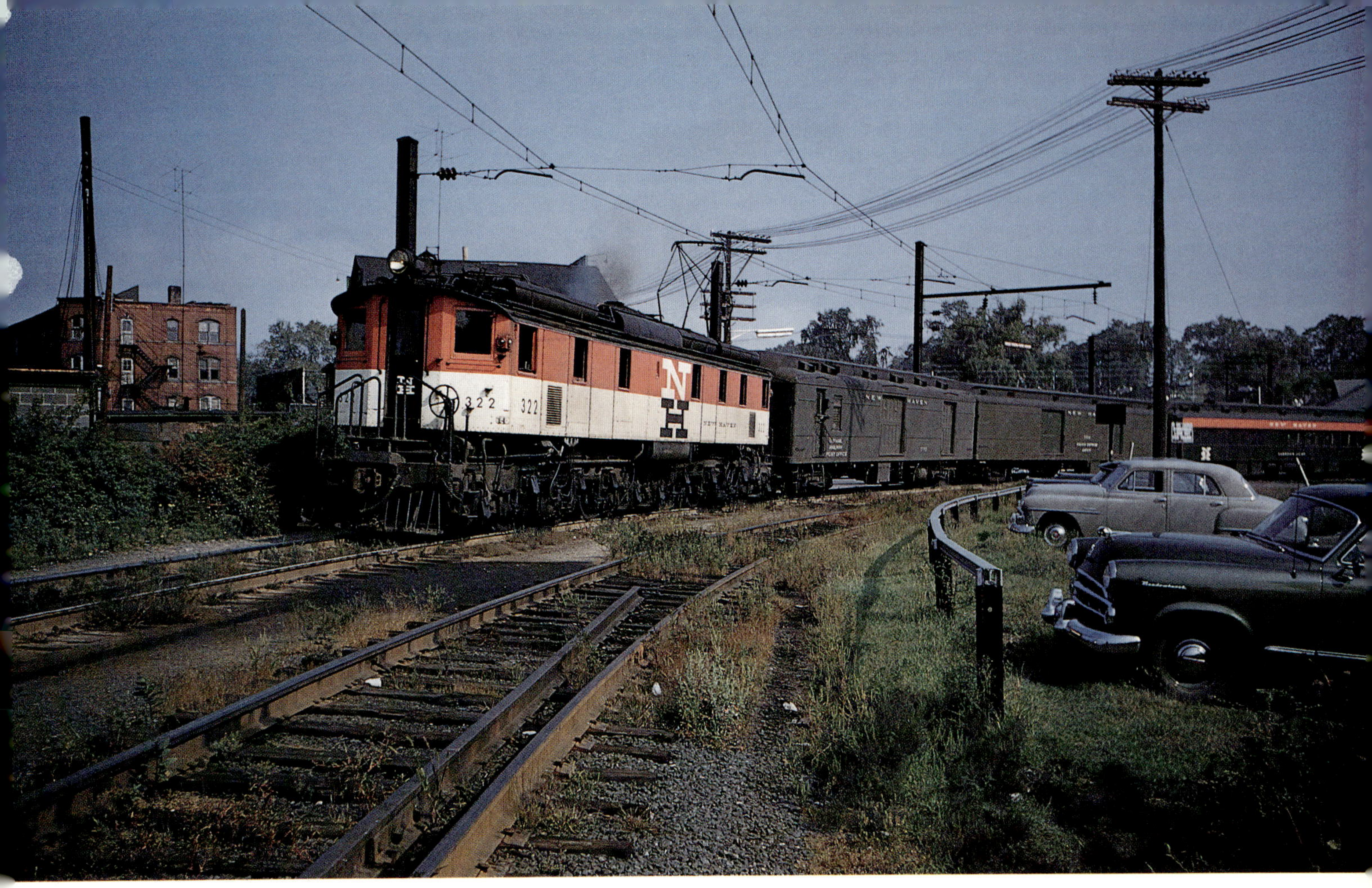
322
322

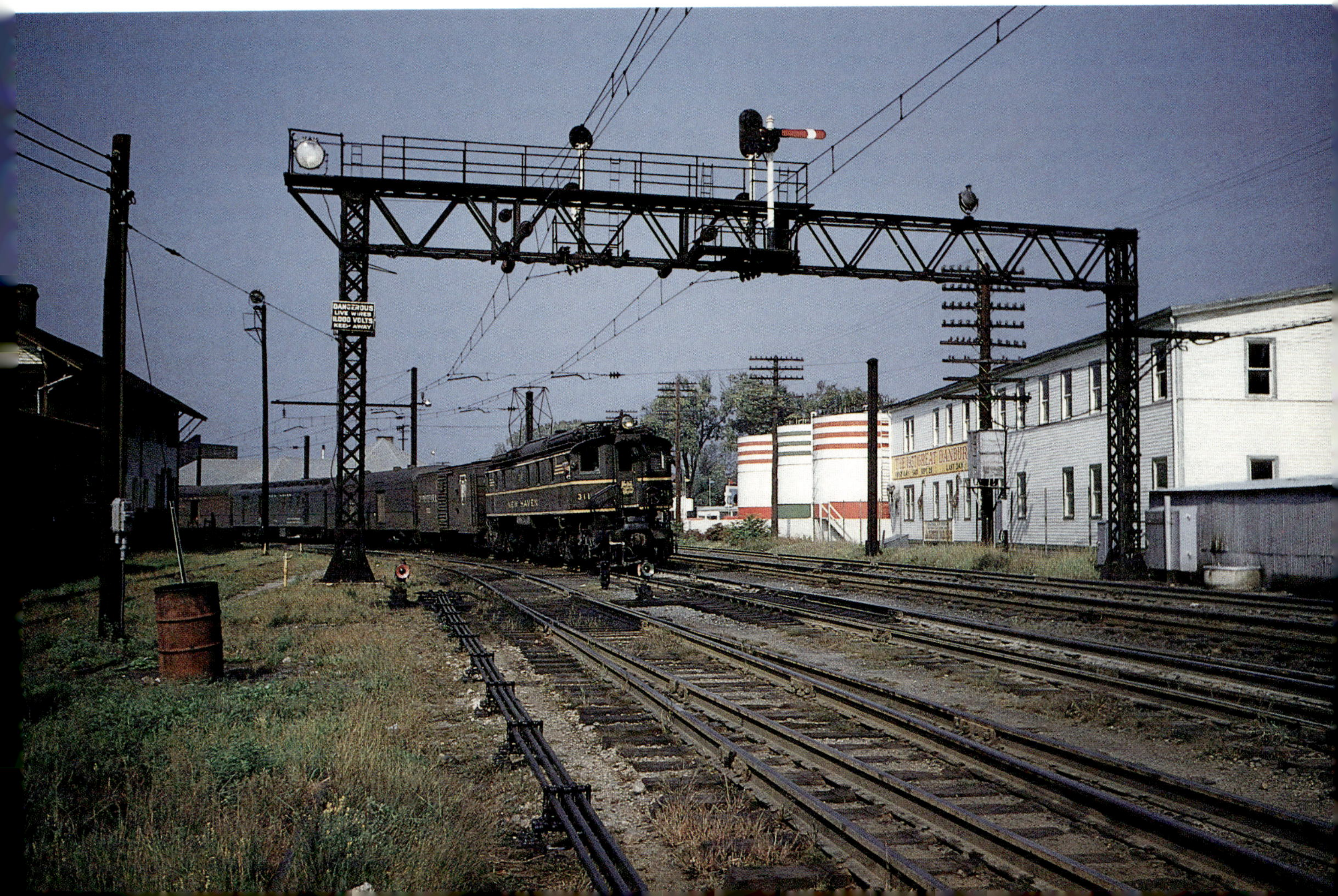
DANGEROUS
LIVE WIRES
11,000 VOLTS
KEEP AWAY

(Above) As motor #311 pulled away from the train, RS3 #561 backed down into view, assigned the task of taking over the run to Pittsfield. *(Opposite page, top)* During the change of power, S-1 #0972 removed a headend mail car for Danbury. *(Opposite page, bottom)* In September 1957, RS3 #525 was covering the south local assignment out of Danbury to South Norwalk. The single track line was electrified with a few passing sidings, also electrified. The RS3 was hustling to clear the main track for train #141 that would be along in about one hour. Judging from the size of the train, there was a good deal of local traffic on the line.

NEW HAVEN
0972

W
NEW HAVEN
525

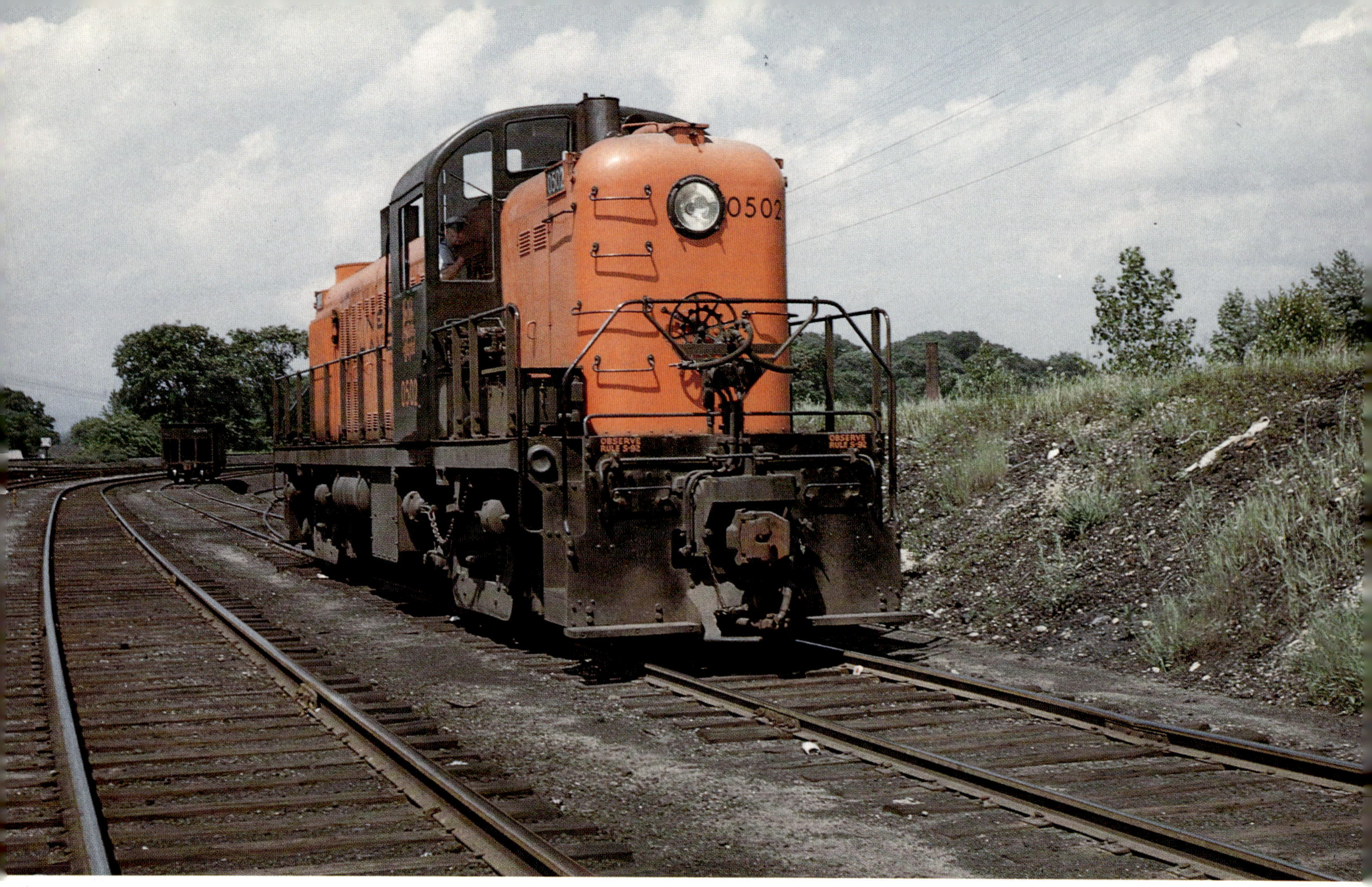
0502

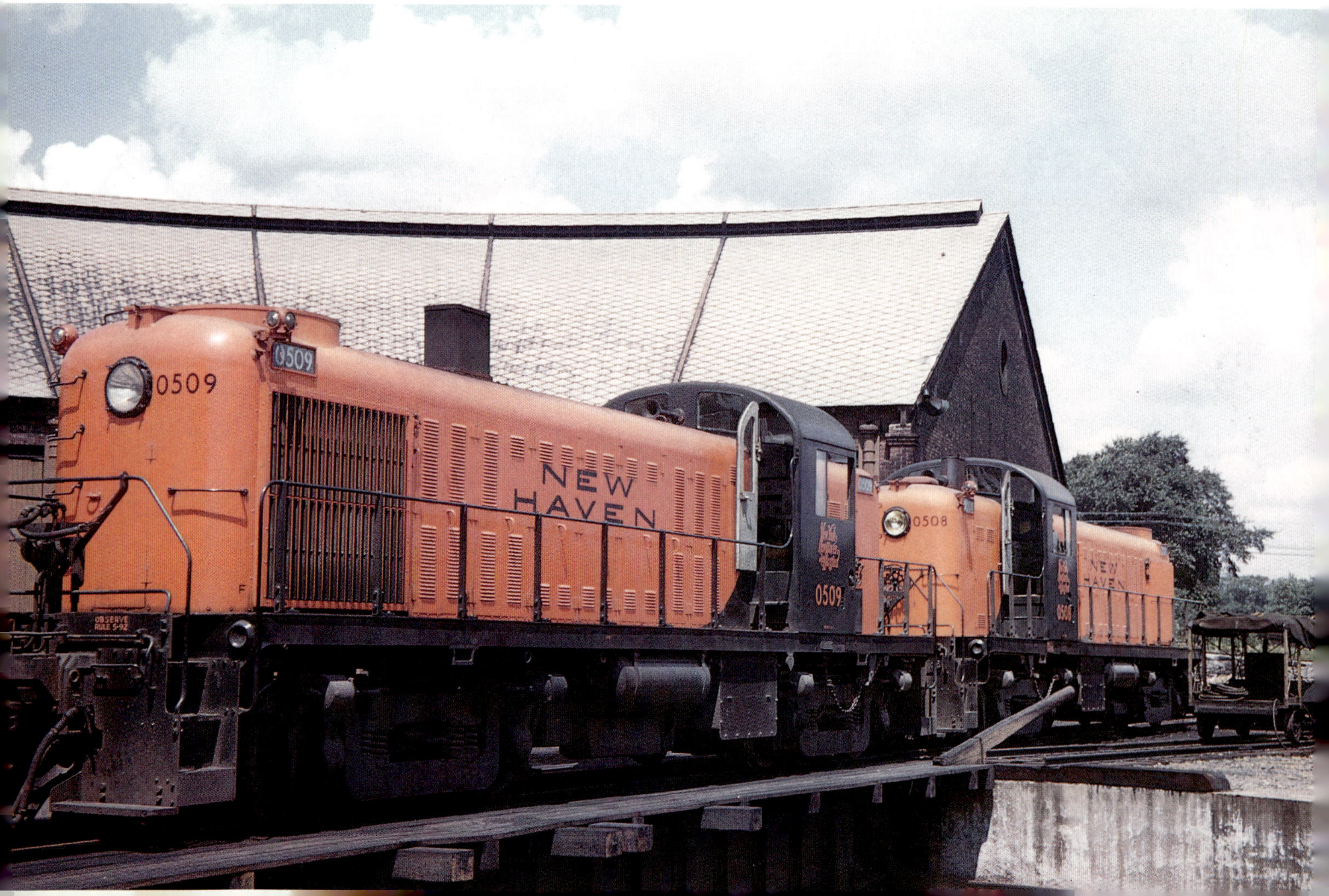
0509
0509
NEW
HAVEN
0509
0508
NEW
HAVEN

Pittsfield, Mass.

In 1947, the New Haven ordered ten RS2's to replace Moguls and Pacifics on the branch from Danbury, Conn. to Pittsfield, Mass. Numbered #0500 to #0509, these RS2's were equipped with steam generators for passenger and freight service. Each day, three RS2's left Danbury with the "Night Freight" RI-2 on its way to Rising and the B&A interchange at State Line. This power was split at State Line for a 6 AM local to Pittsfield and an 8 AM local. After running cab light to Rising, the first local picked up the previously set off traffic for Pittsfield, ran express to Pittsfield to do the industrial switching and performed the southbound local work on their return. The second train did the local work northbound, pulled the outbound loads from the B&A and returned express to Rising. The units from the two locals would be coupled together to form power for IR-1, interchange traffic from the B&A train NH-4 at State Line, going south to Danbury, Norwalk, and Bridgeport. One other local freight north out of Danbury required an RS2. RS2's were also busy handling the two daily except Sunday passenger assignments to Danbury with the trains going on with electrics to New York City. Seven AM train #141 heading south returned as #144 and the morning train #140 that went north from Grand Central returned as train #143 in the afternoon. These four trains all met at Branchville, Conn., 10.8 miles south of Danbury, with the northbound trains taking siding per "right of schedule." On Fridays through Sundays there were extra weekend passenger runs for New Yorkers vacationing in the Berkshires. All of this activity was handled by just one order of 10 RS2's in 1947.

(Above) In June 1948, there were two trains each workday to New York City. #0509 was at Pittsfield, Mass. ready to pull #143 for the four hour trip to New York. The RS2 handled the train to Danbury, Conn., the start of the electrified zone and the change of power. With a 2 PM departure, the passengers would arrive at the *Big Apple* in time for a dinner engagement on Park Avenue. The engine crew turned at Danbury, but the train crew would go through to New York City. Everyday #143 carried an extra express car with paper that had been produced specifically to government specifications for printing money. The paper was carried in wooden chests under armed guards to Washington, D.C. from the Crane Paper Company of Pittsfield. *(Opposite page, top)* With the second local of the morning, #0502 was switching Pittsfield yard in 1948. The local worked seven days per week and pulled the outbound loads from the B&A before returning to Rising. From this view, the buffer casting over the coupler and steam connector were visible for its passenger assignments. Additional passenger air brake valves and signal equipment were located along the fireman's side of the short hood with the long hoods mainly oriented northbound. *(Opposite page, bottom)* #0508 and #0509 were coupled together in 1948 on the armstrong turntable at Pittsfield, a few months after delivery. This original New Haven paint scheme for road switchers included hoods completely painted orange without green stripes and " New Haven" was spelled out in two lines on the long hood. Part of a group of ten RS2's on the New Haven, #0500 to #0509 were delivered from December 1947 to January 1948. The next year seven more RS2's, #0510 to #0516, were delivered in November and December; however, they were not assigned to the Pittsfield line.   *(three photos- Mike Bullock)*

New Haven, Conn.

At New Haven Motor Storage in September 1957, the second set of FL-9's arrived soon after delivery *(above)*. #2002 and #2003 bumped older motors into retirement. The thirty FL-9's in this order were special "F" units equipped for third rail operation into Grand Central Terminal. This first group had a 567C engine rated at 1750hp. In 1960, the New Haven ordered a second group of thirty FL-9's. This batch had a 1800hp 567D engine inside the carbody. All sixty were delivered in McGinnis colors with red on the lowest panels. *(Opposite page, top)* On the same day, EP-3 #358 led a train out of New Haven for Penn Station, New York. #355 and #358 were the only EP-3's painted in the McGinnis colors with white on the lower panels. For years these ten motors were the backbone of the electric passenger fleet. In 1933, #0354 went to the PRR for testing at Claymont, Delaware. It performed so well that it became the prototype for the running gear of the famous GG1. *(Opposite page, bottom)* EP-4 #360 was basically the same motor and wheel arrangement as the EP-3, only on a streamlined carbody. Built by GE in 1938, all but wreck damaged #363 lasted until 1963. *(This page bottom)* This six unit order was later followed by ten similiar freight motors with the same type of streamlining. #360 was renumbered from 366 in 1948 in order to start the group on an even number. The date was September 11, 1957 for the photograph of #360.

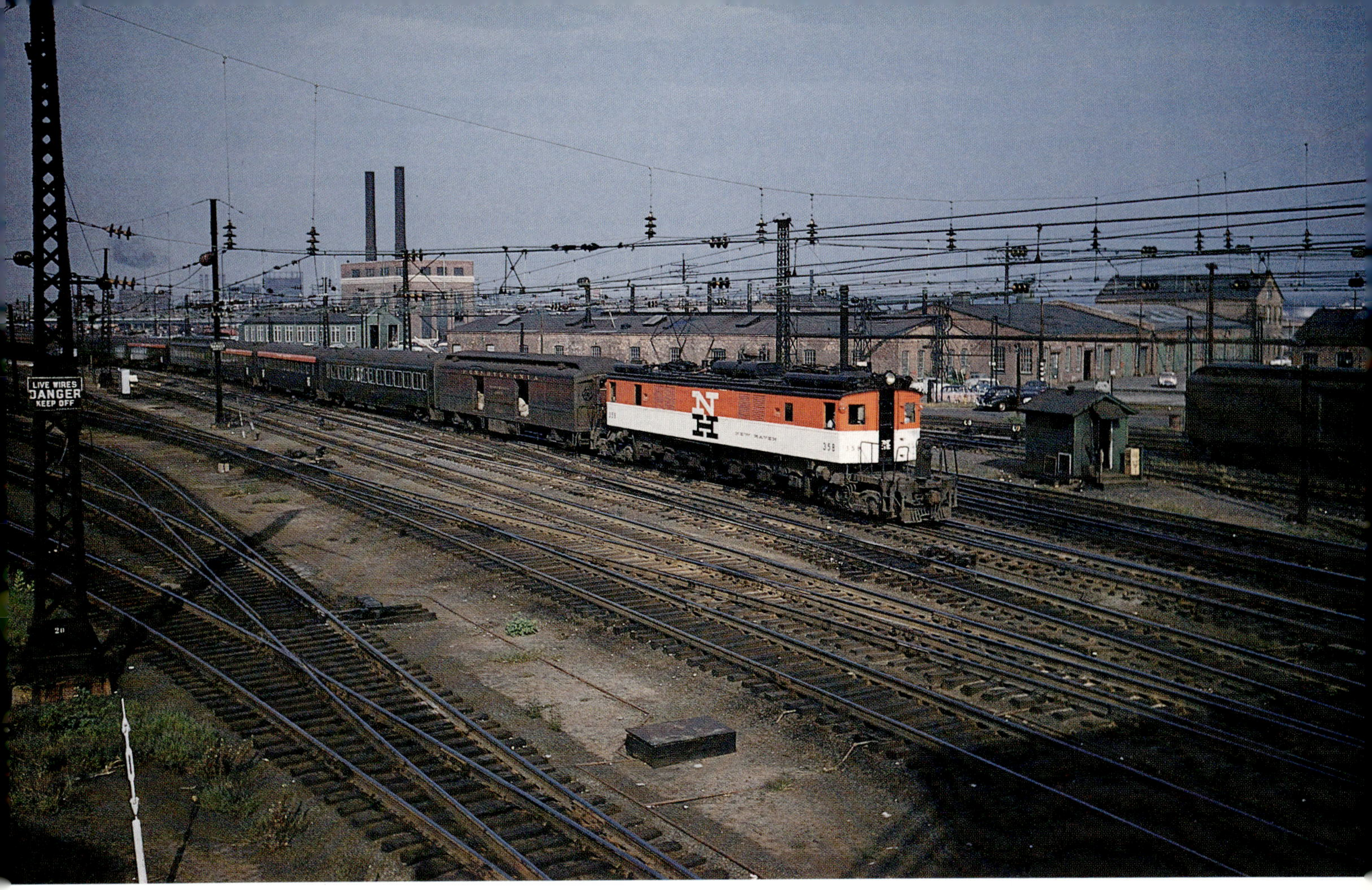
LIVE WIRES
DANGER
KEEP OFF
NH
358

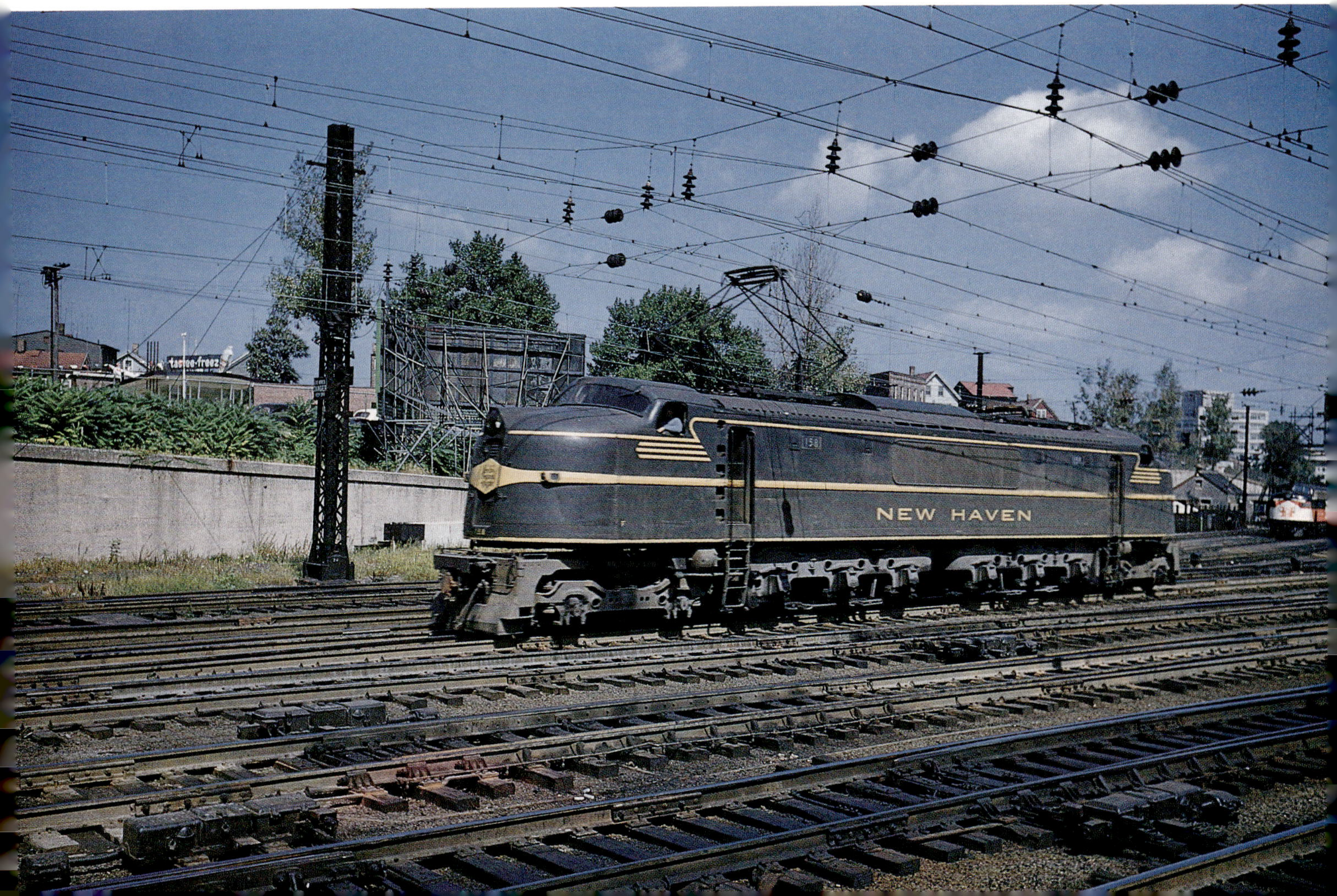
tastee-freez
NEW HAVEN

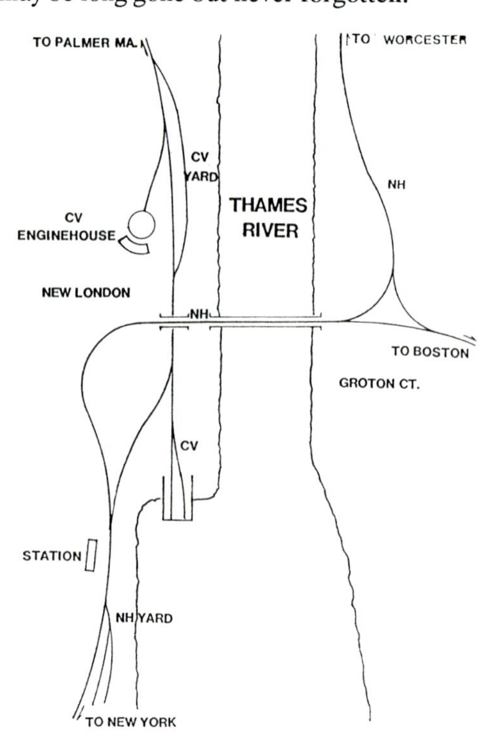

New London, Conn.

(Above) #0732 leads a Shore Line train for Boston through New London. After two blasts on the signal line, the turbochargers of the two units started their high pitched whine to get their engines up to speed for the one hour trip to Providence. From this angle, the modified radiator air flow shutters are clearly visible, a feature designed by the New Haven to improve the performance of the DL109's. It was the summer of 1953 and the 0700's had only a few more summers in mainline service. The Otto Kuhler designed noses may be long gone but never forgotten!

(Opposite page, top) For the "last" last steam trip on the New Haven, #3016 a J-1 class 2-8-2 was used to pull the excursion through New London, Conn. Typical of iron horses, the J-1 takes water before heading north to Putnam, Conn. #3016, built along USRA light 2-8-2 lines, was saved as a snow melter for the New Haven area. Two others, #3006 and 3020, lasted past dieselization to cover the other snow melting assignments of Boston and Providence.

(Opposite page, bottom) Under the New London Route 1 highway bridge, Central Vermont #500 awaited her switching assignment on a cold October morning in 1952. New London was an important interchange with the New Haven and a seaport for coastal shipping. Through the 1940's, CV ships steamed to and from New York City with traffic from Canada. #500 was the first of eight 0-8-0's built by Alco in 1923 along with the 2-8-0's. Purchased and owned by the Canadian National and leased to subsidiary CV, these 0-8-0's were almost identical to the GTW P-5's. All except #504 had Elesco feed water heaters applied. With the delivery of three S-2 Alco diesels in 1941 and 1942, four of these P-1a's were transferred to the CN; the rest lasted right up to dieselization in 1957.   *(Mike Usenia photo DRS collection)*

NEW HAVEN
3016

500

Willimantic, Conn.

In the 1950's, Willimantic was an important crossing of rail lines. Back in 1876, the Air Line Railroad connected New Haven and Willimantic forming an inland route to Boston. At Willimantic this line intersected the Providence to Hartford route of the New Haven and the north-south route of the Central Vermont. This intersection was actually at Bridge Street where a ball signal *(right)* was erected to control traffic. This was one of the first ball signals in the United States. In the early 1950's, a ball signal lighted with lanterns was still controlling traffic at Bridge Street. *(Below)* The street crossing watchman protected the crossing after setting the high ball for the CV local to proceed north to Palmer, Massachusetts. The M-3a class 2-8-0's kept crossing Willimantic for another two years after this July 1955 scene. That 2-8-0 was hurrying to get north as through freight #491 was hot on his trail.

(Opposite page, top) At that time, the Central Vermont was using CN road diesel power on the through trains. On a hot summer day two Canadian built H-16-44's were enroute to Montreal. Only four months old, #1853 and 1854 carried their original numbers on the green and yellow Maple Leaf color scheme. CN only ordered one group of eighteen H-16-44's #1841-1858, which made them difficult to photograph among the engines of the large CN diesel roster. *(Opposite page, center)* With the upper arm of the high ball diagonal and lower arm horizontal, it was OK for the New Haven RDC's to proceed on to Willimantic station and Boston in this April 1954 photo. By the mid-50's, passenger service had ended and Bridge Street would never again see the same variety of activities. *(Opposite page, bottom)* The same day, CV #451, a M-3a 2-8-0 stopped at the high ball with the local going south to New London. One of the six 2-8-0's built by Alco in 1915, before CN control, five of these locomotives were equipped with Coffin feed-water heaters. After the newer N-5a Consolidations were delivered, these 2-8-0's were relegated to local service. By 1954, #451's tender had been cut down to a "clear vision" version to improve the sight line for switching while backing up.

New Haven Employee Timetable No. 175 of April 27 1952, page 88:

BRIDGE STREET - Enginemen of movements to and from Hartford route and C.V. Ry. must sound engine whistle signal 14(m). Enginemen of movements to and from Chestnut Hill route must sound engine whistle signal 14 (q). The indication of the fixed signals governs movements as follows:

-**Proceed, Hartford Route.** By day-Upper arm in diagonal position and lower arm in horizontal position. By night-Two green lights on upper arm in diagonal position and two red lights on lower arm in horizontal position. **Proceed, Chestnut Hill Route.** By day-Upper arm in horizontal position and lower arm in diagonal position. By night-Two green lights on upper arm in horizontal position and two red lights on lower arm in diagonal position. **Proceed, C.V. Ry.** By day-Upper arm in vertical position and lower arm in horizontal position. By night-Two green lights on upper arm in vertical position and two red lights on lower arm in horizontal position. **Stop, all routes.** By day-Both arms in horizontal position. By night-Two green lights on upper arm in horizontal position and two red lights on lower arm in horizontal position.

Monson, Mass.

At the top of State Line Grade, CN FA-1 #9403 powered train #430 on the CV *(above)*. Canadian National FA-1's #9400 to #9407 were frequently assigned to this run. They were built by Montreal Locomotive Works in April through June of 1950 and were the only FA-1's on the CN system. The date was April 16, 1955.

(Opposite page, top) In July of 1954, CN C-liner #8718 headed train #430. South of Monson, Mass., #8718 passed an Alco switcher "holding siding" for the through train. After initial orders for three A units and three B units, CN placed an order for twenty A units model CFA-16-4. The A units carried even numbers and the B units odd numbers. Very conservative on motive power purchases, the CN only obtained the C-liners for freight and passenger service in the 1600hp power range.

(Opposite page, bottom) In April of 1948, M-3a #455 stopped at Monson with the northbound local. At that time, the 2-8-0's still carried a regular tender before being cut down to a clear vision model. #455 was the first of the six M-3a's to be retired and one of the five to be equipped with the distinctive Coffin feed-water heater.
(Mike Bullock photo)

Palmer, Mass.

Palmer, Massachusetts, the crossroads of the Boston and Albany and the Central Vermont, has always been an active railroad town. A CV predecessor line, the New London, Willimantic & Palmer, reached Palmer from New London in 1850 and the line to North Amherst and Belchertown was operating in 1853. This line going north crossed at grade the Western Railroad of Massachusetts, later called the Boston and Albany. *(Above)* #472 pounded over the B&A diamond on her way with the south end local. It was a cold January day in 1954 with a little snow on the ground. The 2-8-0 lost her footing on the frost covered rails as the engineer tried to clear the crossing before stabbing a B&A freight. These M-5a's would be around Palmer three more years before being replaced by GP9's. *(Below)* In September 1954, RS3 #8223 led a local passenger train with many head end cars. The two RS3's were accelerating the train just west of the CV diamond, their 244's revved up producing black smoke. Five RS3's leading heavy B&A passenger trains were not uncommon during the early fifties. #8223 was the first of over one hundred RS3's purchased by the NYC and used extensively on the east end of the system.

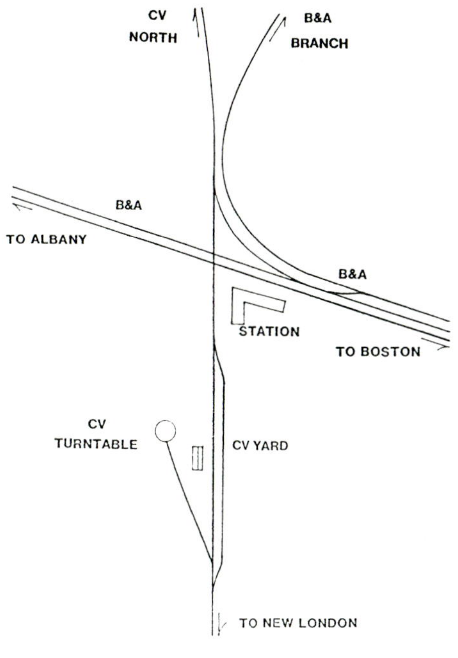

(Above) In March 1949, M-2a #402 was moving off the turntable at Palmer. The CV facility was a small wooden coaling chute next to the turntable and a water tank for servicing the local's power north and south. The fireman watched carefully as the engine backed off the table, preparing for the run north to Brattleboro, Vermont. In 1928 when the CV received the 2-10-4's for the north end, older 2-8-0's #405 to #418 were returned to the Canadian National leaving only #400 to #404 of the M-2a's on the CV. Built by Alco in 1905, these smaller 2-8-0's would soon be retired. *(Below)* #463 raced through Monson, Ma., just south of Palmer, preparing for the grade to the Massachusetts/Connecticut State line. Train #430 had connecting traffic for New London from Montreal. Most of the time, traffic was heavy enough for two M-5a's on the point. It was beautiful weather on this August day in 1949, long before the thought of diesels on this run.

(Both photos by Mike Bullock)

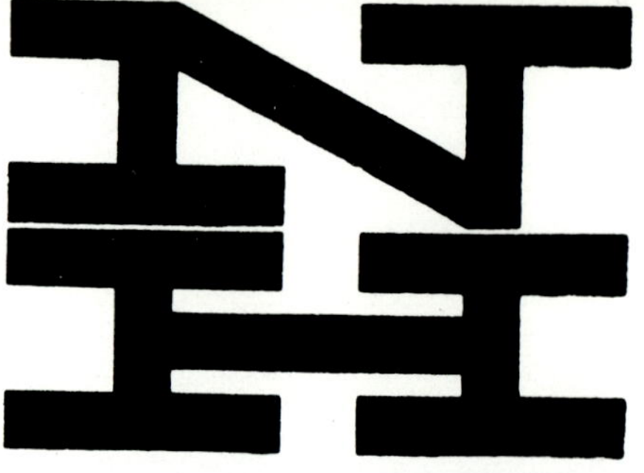

Worcester, Mass.

Worcester, Massachusetts was the crossroads of the B&A, B&M, and New Haven railroads. In October 1847, the Providence and Worcester opened service into town and later, in 1892, leased operations to the New Haven for 99 years. *(Above)* In August of 1962, Boston and Maine GP9 #1710 led a camper extra into the New Haven yard. Returning empty from Maine, the Pullmans went through to New York City. #1710 was one of fifty GP9's built from FT trade-in material in 1957. Unfortunately, #1710 was wrecked on the Penn Central eleven years after manufacture and removed from the roster. *(Opposite page, top)* Carrying the same train, New Haven H-16-44 #1604 was part of a 1956 fifteen unit order for the model to be used both in passenger and freight service. With a Train Master styled car body and GE electrical equipment, these units lasted into the Penn Central era. *(Opposite page, bottom)* #0416 FA-1 waited for her assignment at New Haven's Worcester enginehouse in the later colors of red orange and black. This FA-1 was not one of the eight units remanufactured by Alco, upgraded to 1600hp, equipped with nose MU, and capable of MU'ing with the newer units.

(Above) In 1953, the NEW ENGLAND STATES was the finest train on the Boston and Albany. #4500 led an all FM consist powering the Budd built stainless steel equipment west of Worcester. It was a *Consolidated Line* unit, CPA-24-5, standing for C-line, passenger A unit, 2400hp, five axles. The extra axle was needed to support the weight of the steam generator and water tank. Built by FM in 1952, it was the first of eight units of its type on the NYC. The second unit was a 4400 series "Erie built" A unit, rated at 2000hp. In the early years of dieselization, the B&A was home for several of the FM cab units, both freight and passenger. For New England, FM styled cab units powered trains on the Boston & Albany, Central Vermont, and New Haven. The Candian Pacific also owned some, but they rarely ran over lines in New England.

(Opposite page, top) Anywhere on the B&A was a good location to see the largest fleet of Alco freight cabs in the U.S. Late in the afternoon in September 1962, five FA's accelerated a westbound freight after a pickup at Worcester. Their 244 diesel engines smoked up the air a bit while getting up to speed. #1043 was still in lightning stripes leading four black "FB" units. #1043 was the last built of 44 FA-1's on the NYC roster, part of almost 200 FA's owned by them. The low camera angle and clear sky enhanced the classic lines of the FA consist.

(Opposite page, bottom) RDC's from the Boston & Maine and New Haven met at Worcester station in July 1958. The NH RDC-1 was waiting for a Worcester to New London assignment and the B&M RDC-1 was laying over during a passenger extra run. The New Haven operated forty RDC's and the B&M over one hundred by the end of the 1950's.

Belchertown, Mass.

Belchertown was ten miles north of Palmer on the Central Vermont. The B&M, Central Massachusetts branch, also used the CV line for 8.3 miles through Belchertown. *(Above)* On a cool sunny day, the last day of March 1955, the southbound CV local "took siding" for the westbound B&M local. As CV 2-8-0 #453 pulled down to clear, the B&M Alco waited on the main. CV work cars were in abundance to haul ties for the siding extension at Amherst. Longer trains and diesel operation soon followed. *(Opposite page, top)* Six months earlier, in October 1954, M-5a #468 placed the work train on the siding. The brakeman was about to throw the switch to clear the main as the 2-8-0 moved down past the clearance point. It was a beautiful, warm and clear fall day in Belchertown. By the looks of this M-5a, the CV was still keeping its 2-8-0's in good mechanical condition. These 2-8-0's were dual service locomotives, good for 55 mph in passenger operation. *(Opposite page, bottom)* Once the main was cleared, train #430 arrived on its southbound trip from Montreal with two C-liners on the head end. #8708 was part of the November 1952 order for twenty CFA-16-4's, 1600hp, four axle, cab "A" units, built by Canadian Locomotive Company. During the early fifties, CN supplied diesel power for train #430 and #490, mainly FM and Alco styled cabs.

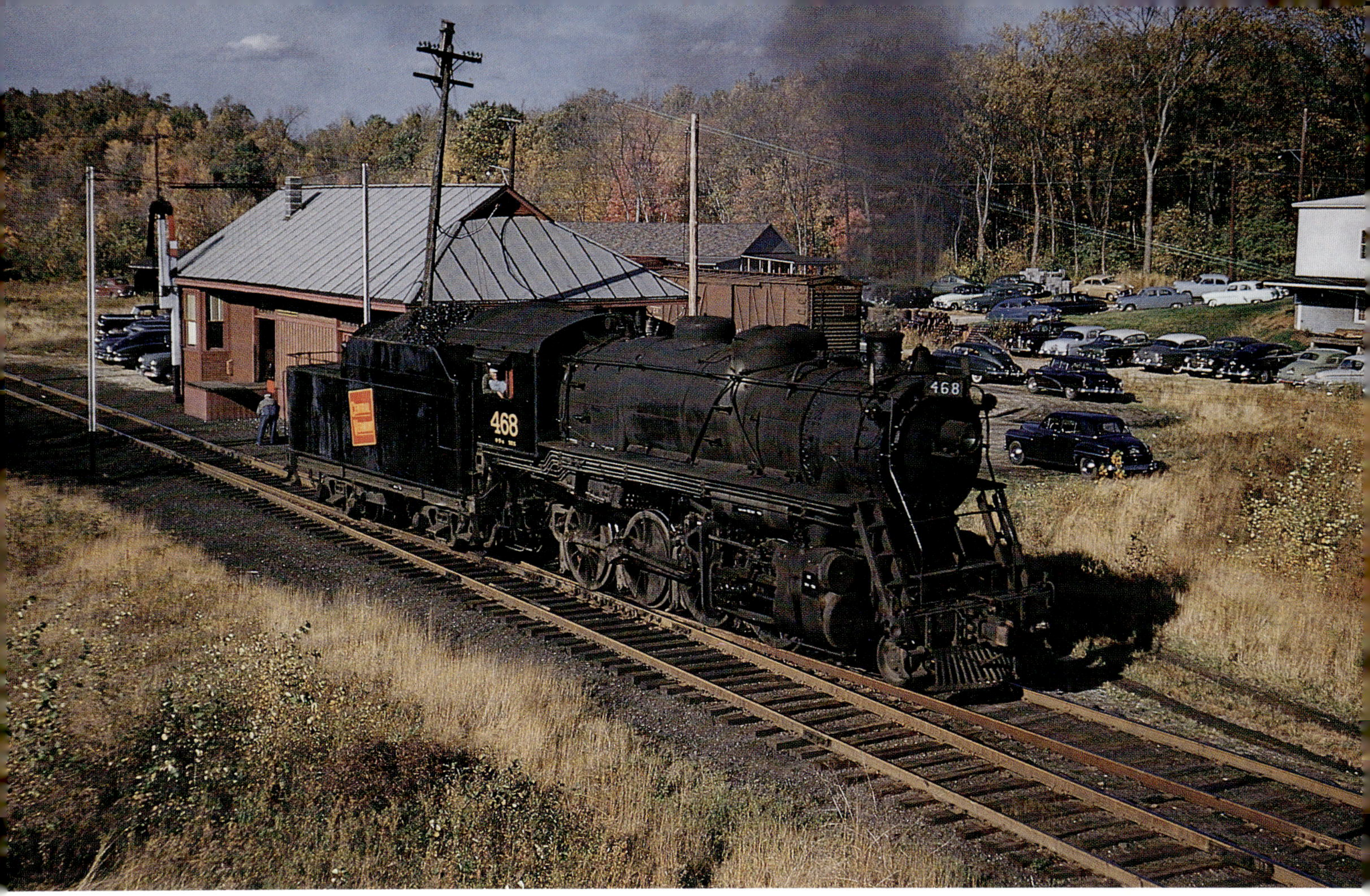
468
468

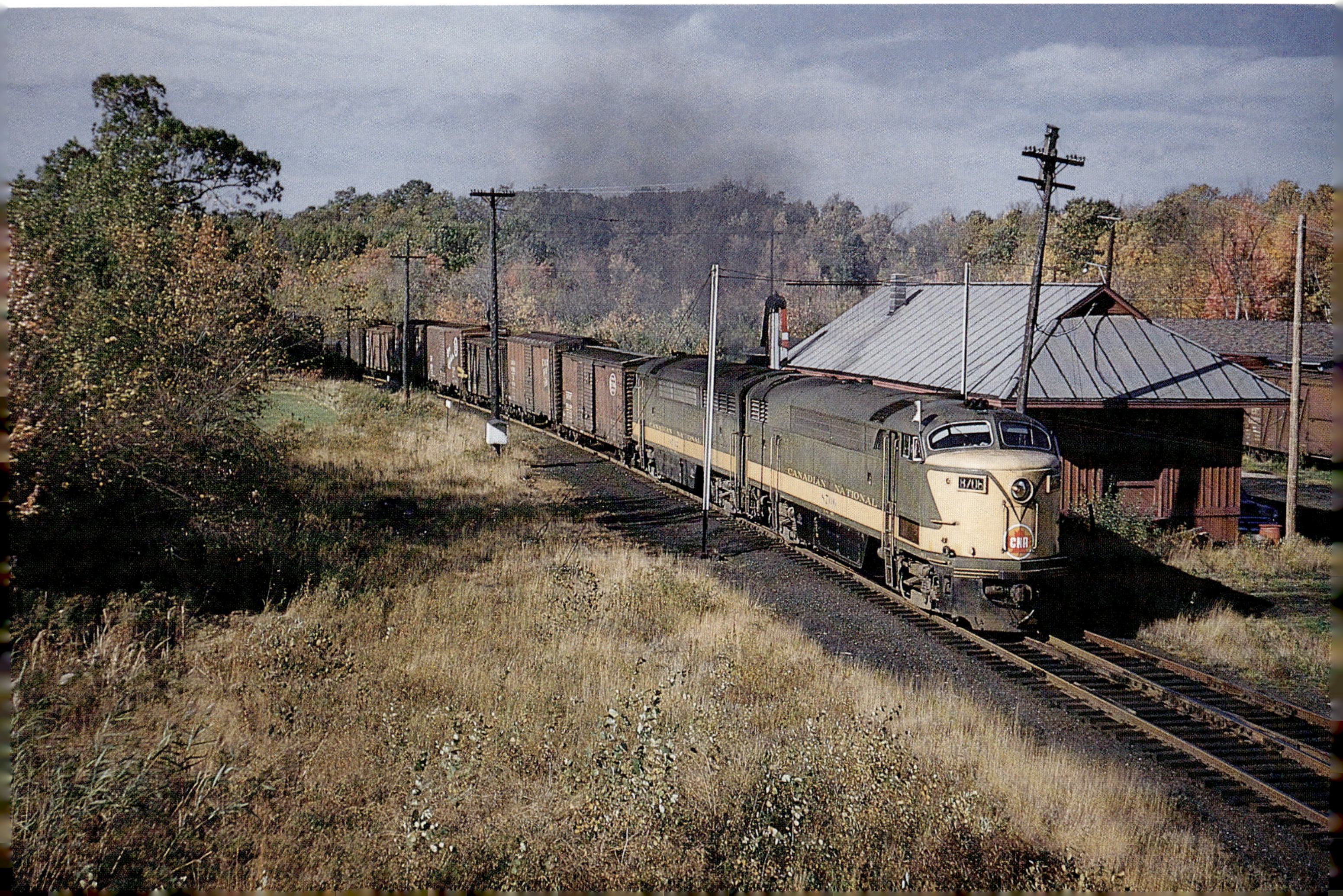
CANADIAN NATIONAL
CNR

Bellows Falls, Vt.

Bellows Falls, Vermont was the crossing of the Rutland line with the Connecticut River Line. The river line at this point was a joint CV/B&M operation. *(Above)* In June of 1956, a southbound train led by #4227 A & B passed through Bellows Falls on its way to Springfield, Mass. and New York City. Three balls exposed on the high ball meant "clear" for the Connecticut River Line and the operator handed up orders to the crew on the head end. In 1948 the B&M purchased two A-B sets of F3's for passenger service. Delivered as late F3's in the fall of 1948, the units looked like F7's and were often referred to as F5's. *(Below)* #1173, an S3, switched the B&M yard just over the river in New Hampshire on the line to Boston. #1173 was the first of sixteen S3's on the B&M built during the 1950-1952 period of time. *(Opposite page)* One ball meant the arrival of the Rutland freight crossing the diamond on the way to the B&M yard. Once at Walpole, N.H., RS3 #208 dropped its train and returned to Rutland with B&M interchange traffic. #208 was the last of nine RS3's delivered to the Rutland. The last group of four RS3's, #205 to #208, could always be identified from the rest with the addition of dual sealed beam headlights. After the downfall of the Rutland Railway in 1961, these RS3's went to work for the Louisville & Nashville.

RUTLAND
RAILROAD

GREEN MT.
RUTLAND
GATEWAY

Rutland, Vt.

A group of small Vermont railroads were consolidated to form the Rutland Railway in 1901. Its name sake, Rutland, Vermont, was the hub of the operation. After only four years with four modern 4-8-2's, the Rutland management decided to dieselize the railroad. In January 1951, Alco RS3 demonstrator #1601 tested on the Rutland. It was later purchased and renumbered #200. This unit was shortly followed by a second RS3 #201 to start the dieselization process.

(Above) RS3 #202 was at the Rutland diesel shop in July of 1959. #202 was part of a 1951 order for three RS3's #202-204. The generally good condition of #202 and the shop facility would not indicate that the railroad would be shut down within two years and that #202 would head for South Louisville, Ky. shops.

(Opposite page, top) On the same day, 70 tonner #500 was switching Rutland yard. They had ordered one 70 tonner in 1951 to replace the steam switcher at the yard.

(Opposite page, bottom) One year earlier in 1958, 70 tonner #500 moved #401 at the diesel shop. RS1's #400-405 were the remaining element of the 1951 diesel order. Thus nine RS3's, six RS1's, and one 70 tonner replaced 52 steam locomotives between 1950 and 1952 on the Rutland.

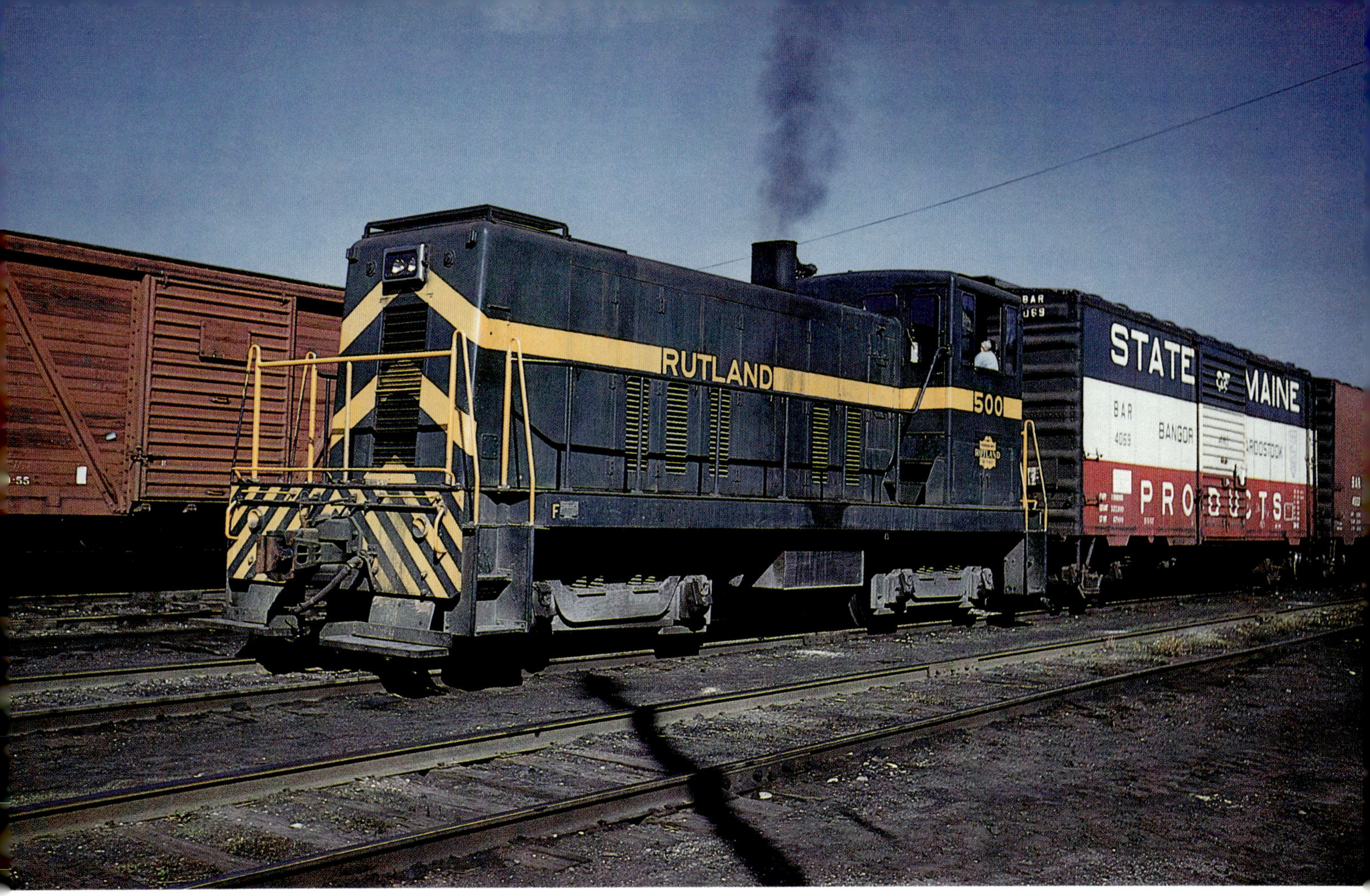
RUTLAND
500
STATE
MAINE

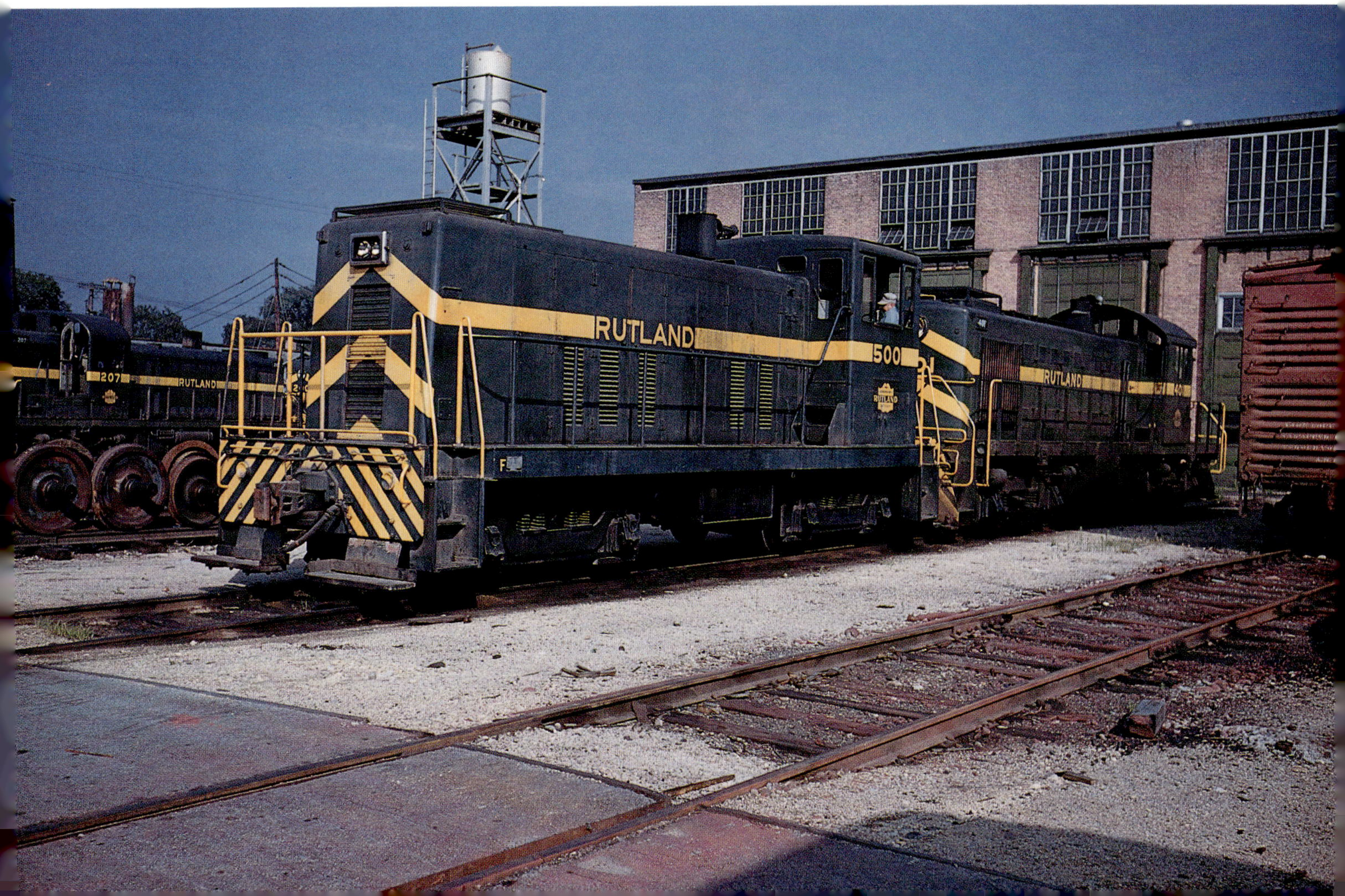
RUTLAND
500
RUTLAND
207
RUTLAND

Springfield, Vt.

North of Bellows Falls was the small town of Springfield, Vermont, the machine tool capital of New England. In 1897 the Springfield Electric Railway, later Springfield Terminal, started operating from Charlestown, N.H. to Springfield, Vt. Passenger trolley service ended in January 1947; however, electric freight service continued to serve the machine tool industry until October of 1956. *(Above)* Freight was interchanged with the Boston & Maine Connecticut River Line at the Springfield station in New Hampshire. *(Below)* On June 20, 1956 steeple cab motor #20 picked up two cars off the interchange track. After a safety inspection and an air test by the crew, it was a quick trip to town with only two loads. #20 was a 50 ton Baldwin-Westinghouse motor which was built in 1929. *(Opposite page, top)* The Springfield line followed Route 11 straight into Clinton Street. *(Opposite page, bottom)* While crossing South Street at the center of town, all highway traffic was required to stop. The fireman and engineer were ever vigilant for fast moving motorists while negotiating the city streets.

READING

S.T.R.C.
20
SUNOCO
SOUTH ST

B.T.C.
20
16
16
16 
16

B&M
READING

(Above) Six months before de-electrification, the end of the line was the faded wooden Mineral Street barn with the machine tool works in the background.

(Opposite page, top) Sitting at the barn was combine #16 which was no longer needed for passenger service and had been converted to a work car. This 41' steel combine was built in 1926 by Wason along with sister #17 already scrapped.

(Opposite page, bottom) After uncoupling the road power, the crew moved to #15 to switch out the two cars from the rear. This only other motor was manufactured by Baldwin-Westinghouse in 1923. It also was a 50 ton model B-1 and was later sold to the Cornwall Railroad of Canada. Interesting to note that MU equipped #20 could not MU with #15 as this unit was never equipped to multiple. #15 normally did the switching duties around the tool industry in Springfield.

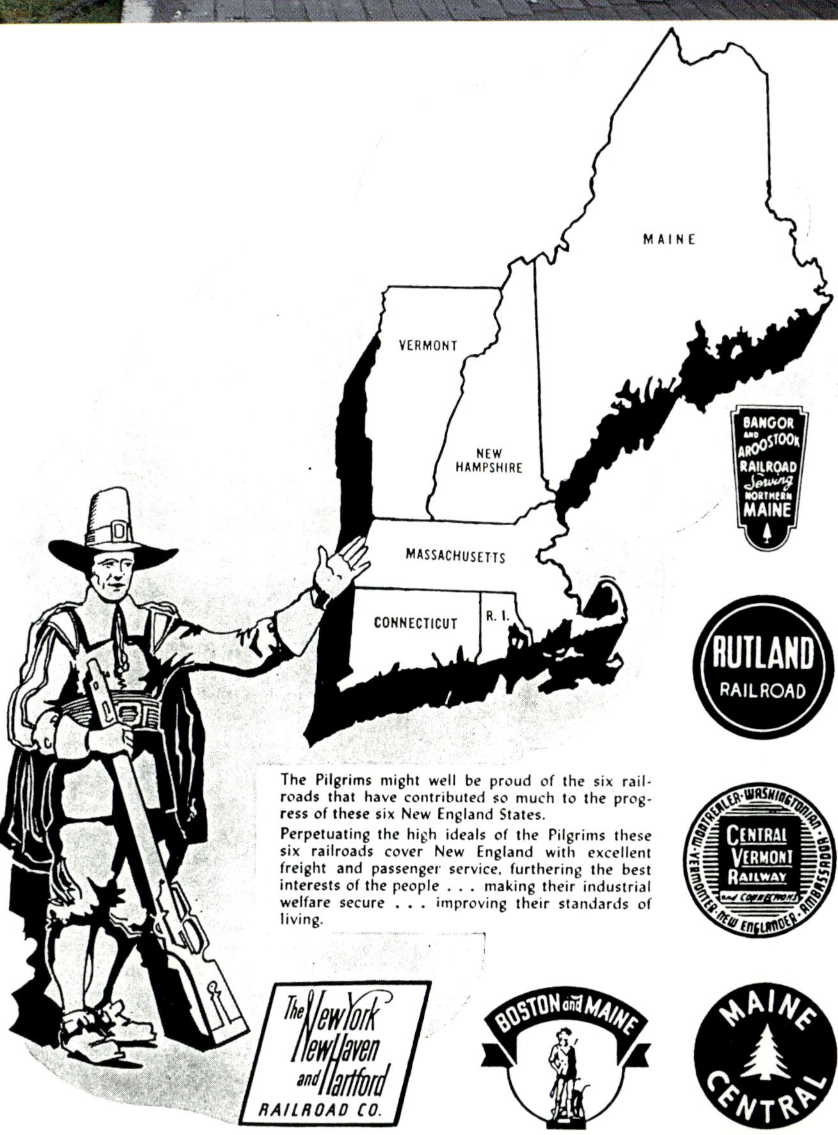

White River Jct., Vt.

White River Jct., Vermont, the town situated at the junction of the White and Connecticut Rivers, became a railroad town with the arrival of train service from Concord, N.H. in 1847. One year later, the predecessor to the CV, the Vermont Central Railroad started operations into town from the south. White River Jct. was always the division point between the Northern and Southern Divisions of the CV and a major connection with the B&M. South of town, the Connecticut River Line had been operated jointly under B&M control the entire distance to East Northfield, Mass. In 1924 through service was inaugurated between Montreal and Washington, D.C. using the B&M/CV through White River Jct. These through trains, the MONTREALER and WASHINGTONIAN, were famous for bootlegging during prohibition. The present colonial styled station building was opened in 1938 with a distinctive locomotive weathervane on the roof. Coming south from Newport, Vt., the Canadian Pacific entered White River Jct. via joint trackage with the B&M running from Wells River, Vt. The B&M handled all passenger trains south to Springfield, Mass. and onto New York City via the New Haven. Also, the B&M handled all passenger service east via Concord, N.H. to Boston.

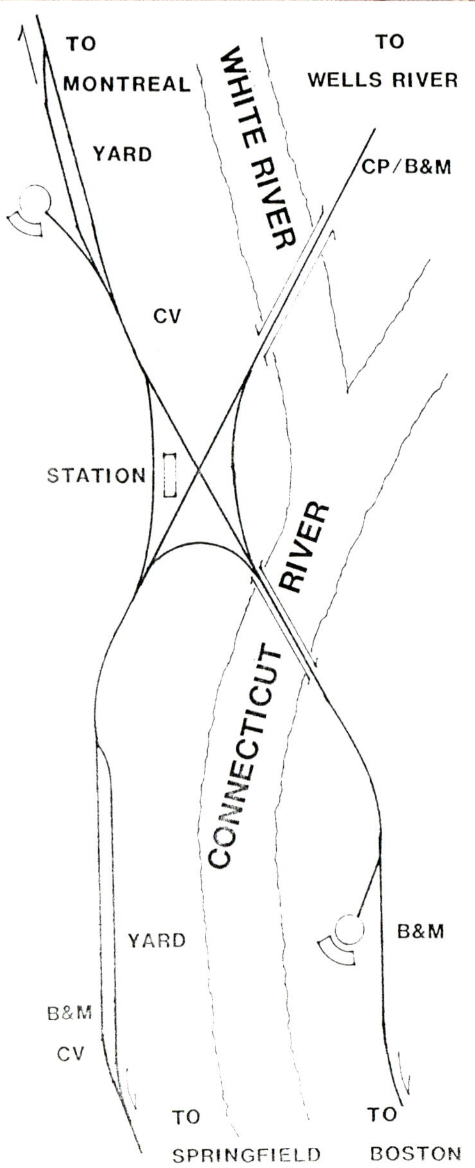

If a railfan with a 35mm camera needed a place to go in northern New England for a wide selection of motive power and railroads, White River Jct. would have been the place! With CV, CN, B&M, and CP road power in a variety of greens and reds, the combinations were unlimited and steam was a frequent visitor to the Junction until mid 1957. *(Opposite page)* For White River Jct., dieselization started early with the assignment of an Alco S2 to the passenger switching operations at the outbreak of World War II. Twenty four years later, #8094 was still going strong waiting to switch a B&M passenger train at the station during the next to last year of passenger service in 1965. *(This page, above)* Under the CV coaling dock was the largest steam power in New England, a CV 2-10-4. Built in 1928, these ten seven hundreds were large by New England standards, but small compared to others of their wheel arrangement. With small 60" drivers, the top speed was limited to 35 mph; however, a few were rebalanced to 43 mph. The CN influence was indicated by the handsome Vanderbilt tenders and all weather cabs. #703 was photographed on February 12, 1955. Also obtained under CN control were four lean and racy 4-8-2's *(below)*. Purchased by the Canadian National in 1927 and leased to the CV, these Mountains were built to a standard Alco light 4-8-2 design similar to the ones owned by the Florida East Coast. Here the CN influence was in the outside-bearing pilot trucks, the same pilot truck as used on their 6000 Mountain class. These race horses were assigned to the MONTREALER and WASHINGTONIAN between White River Jct. and Montreal.

By 1965, some locomotive swapping was taking place among the Canadian National's three U.S. roads. Several CV GP9's were transferred to the Grand Trunk Western and an equal number of RS11's were conveyed to the CV from the Duluth, Winnipeg & Pacific Railway. Under the Green Mountain coaling tower, stood one of these DW&P Alco units *(above)* side by side with CV #4929. The family ties were clearly visible in the common CN paint scheme. *(Below)* The 4900s were passenger numbers for the Geeps of the GTW, GT and CV equipped with roof mounted air tanks, but without dynamic braking. Delivered in December of 1957, this was the last unit to complete dieselization on the Central Vermont. Unfortunately, the unit was later wrecked only to be scrapped in 1973.

Just across the river on the New Hampshire side was the B&M engine facility. All CP and B&M power was serviced at this point, sometimes in mixed combinations. CP dieselized its operations early in 1949 with Alco cabs on the through freights and RS2's on the locals. The famous BL2's covered some of the B&M assignments out of White River in the early 1950's, later giving way to RS3's and F7's. *(Above)* BL2 #1553 was retired in September of 1959, and traded in on a new GP18 in 1961. Totaling four in number, these BL2's never were equipped with MU which shortened their active service to only eleven years. *(Below)* After the arrival of the RDC fleet, most of the B&M RS3's made the Connecticut River their stomping ground. #1540 was one of the eleven Phase II RS3's delivered in 1952.

Even the original B&M 1200, a 1941 vintage NW2, covered the White River switching duties in the late 1960's. In the background *(above)*, the White River Jct. station indicated the wind direction with the famous locomotive weather-vane.

(Opposite page, top) #4265 was one of the very few F7A units built in 1949 for the Boston & Maine. Of the 79 F's on the B&M only eight, four A and four B, were F7's, not the usual ratio for such a popular EMD model.

(Opposite page, bottom) Back in the summer of '56, F2 freight unit #4256 was coupled up to FT set #4222 A & B. The F2 wore another of the experimental McGinnis paint jobs. The 4250 group of F2A units divided some FT's into 3 unit sets when they were delivered in the summer of 1946. Even though the FT's looked very shabby, they never received a coat of blue paint, because within the year they were traded in on new <u>blue</u> GP9's.
(Ralph Phillips photo, DRS collection)

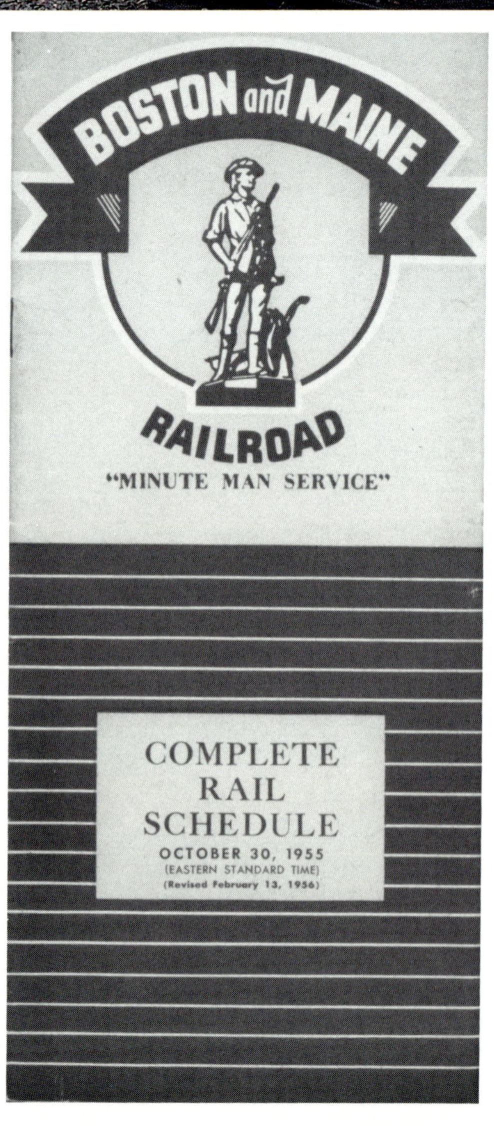

In later years, Canadian Pacific RS10's and RS18's covered most of the road assignments. The CP RS10's *(left)* numbered in the 8400s and 8500s were a Canadian only version of an RS11 styled unit with a 1600hp model 244 engine inside, the same diesel engine that powered the RS3's. The RS10's were a transition unit between the RS3 and the Canadian RS18.

(Below) RS10 #8592 hammered across the diamond at the station in May of 1966 on its way to the south end of town. With script lettering, the unit was set up for operating long hood front. The gray nose always indicated which end was front on the CP units.

Heading north out of White River at Newbury, Vermont, RS18 #8759 *(above)* led a northbound freight. With Alco model 251 1800hp diesel engines, the Canadian RS18's were a far superior locomotive to the trailing RS10. The gray front indicates short hood front operation for the RS18's. *(Below)* Canadian Pacific RS3 #8434 was waiting for her northbound assignment at the B&M engine terminal. Similiar to a U.S. RS3, the Canadian version had a few additional modifications for cold weather operation, the winterization hatch and the carbody filters.

St. Johnsbury, Vt.

St. Johnsbury, Vermont was the junction of the Maine Central, the Canadian Pacific, and the St. Johnsbury and Lamoille County railroads. In 1926, the Canadian Pacific started to run through town when it picked up the lease from the Boston & Maine for the Wells River to Newport, Vermont line. This line from White River Jct. to Newport thus became a joint B&M/CP operation. *(Above)* One of the original RS2's, #8400 dieselized the line in 1949. It was switching St. Johnsbury twenty years later, now sporting her third color scheme. The unit was easily identified as an RS2 with the fuel fill on the cab side just under the number 8400. *(Below)* Sister 8402 was still in the standard maroon and gray scheme as she prepared to handle the local north to Newport. #8402 had additional fuel tanks on either side of the short hood and a modified hand brake.

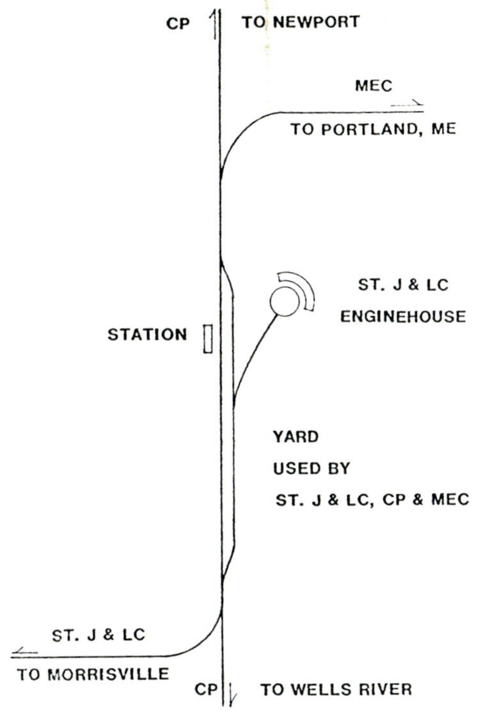

This day *(above)* the northbound freight was led by FP7 #4068, which was part of a group of FP7's built by GMD in London, Ontario in August 1952. General Motors cab units were not common on CP's Vermont operation. Against the gray building skyline of St. Johnsbury, this classic F unit was in script lettering with the beaver crest on the nose. #4068 still had an operating steam generator for occasional passenger assignments. *(Below)* Between the two FP7's was positioned another RS10. But wait! RS10 #8824 was a special single unit order. In 1957, wreck damaged FA1 #4016 was sent to MLW to utilize the diesel engine, main generator, trucks, etc. for the building of a new RS10 long past the end of RS10 production and numbered between GP9's.

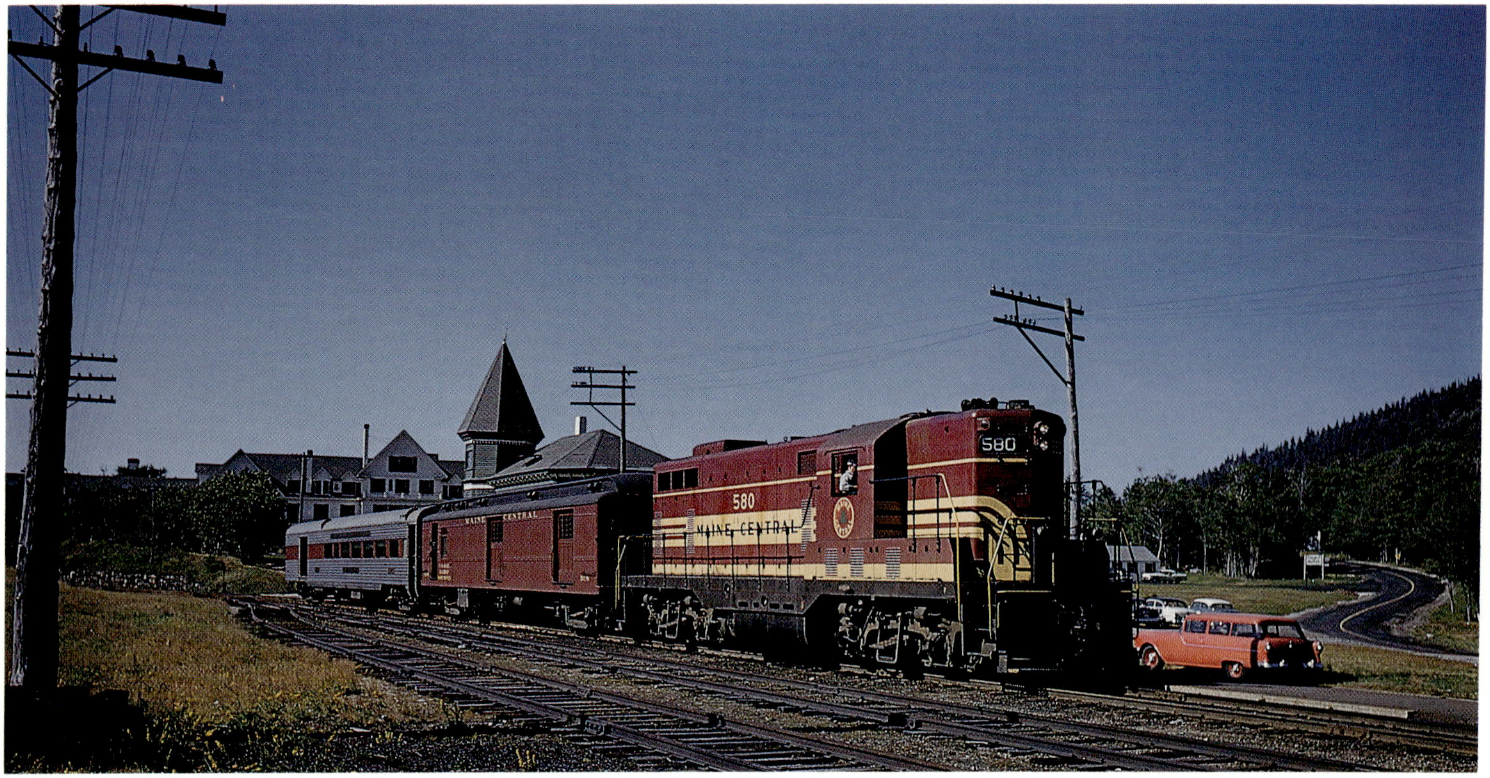

The Maine Central Mountain Division included the famous Crawford Notch. Back in August 1957, when the MEC was still running passenger service between St. Johnsbury and Portland, Maine, GP7 #580 stopped at Crawford Notch station *(above)* for a passenger before the long descent down the mountain. *(Below)* As she departed with her two car consist, the famous Notch came into view. The Pullman Standard stainless steel clad combine was more than adequate for the few passengers making the scenic trip.

In October 1967, one year old Maine Central GP38 #261 *(above)* had completed a trip over the Mountain Division to St. Johnsbury. This was one of the first low-nosed yellow units on the MEC. #251-262 were followed by one more GP38, #263, in the fall of 1967. With the St. J & LC enginehouse in the background, #261 led a group of GP7's into town on this fall day. *(Below)* Turning the clock back to July 1949, B&M RS2 #1504 was about to depart the passenger station for a trip to White River Jct. #1504 was delivered four months earlier, part of a group of nine RS2's delivered in 1949. Soon there were two blasts on the signal line and the 244 prime mover roared into action rolling the milk cars toward White River Jct.

(Bottom- Mike Bullock photo)

1535
1535
BOSTON MAINE

540
CANADIAN PACIFIC 4404
F

Newport, Vt.

In 1948, the CP decided to dieselize the Wells River to Newport operation in Vermont rather than rebuild the bridges and turntable to accommodate heavier steam locomotives. For the diesel operation, it was determined that three 2000hp passenger units would be needed to cover the daytime train the ALOUETTE between Montreal and Boston, the nightime train the REDWING and the "Newport Local." B&M passenger power would be assigned to the run on alternate days for the ALOUETTE. Twelve cabs, five roadswitchers and three switchers were determined as necessary to dieselize the freight operations. After bids were received from all four major builders, Alco got the order because their RS2 road switcher would handle a 3000 pound-per-hour steam generator, was lower priced, and guaranteed faster delivery. The passenger unit order went to EMD to match the B&M E7's already in passenger service. Actually, between the order of 1948 and the delivery in 1949, the model was changed from E7's to E8's because in the new year the model changed radically.

(Above) At Newport, Vermont in October 1963, joint B&M-CP operation was duly recorded. Part of the original RS2 order of 1948, #8403 was waiting for assignment to the southbound local. The winterization hatch over the radiator had been added after delivery to keep the engineroom warm during extreme winter operations, a necessary measure for the cold climate.

(Opposite page) Two Boston & Maine RS3's coupled up with a CP "B" unit to form an all Alco consist. #1535 and 1540 are RS3's from the 1952 B&M order and used extensively on this line. Trailing the road switchers was #4404, a 1950 FB1 from Montreal Locomotive Works: as a matter of record, the very first FB1 built in Canada. On June 16, 1950 FA1 #4008 and the 4404 were delivered, the first Canadian built streamlined road units. Here again the winterization hatch was added after delivery.

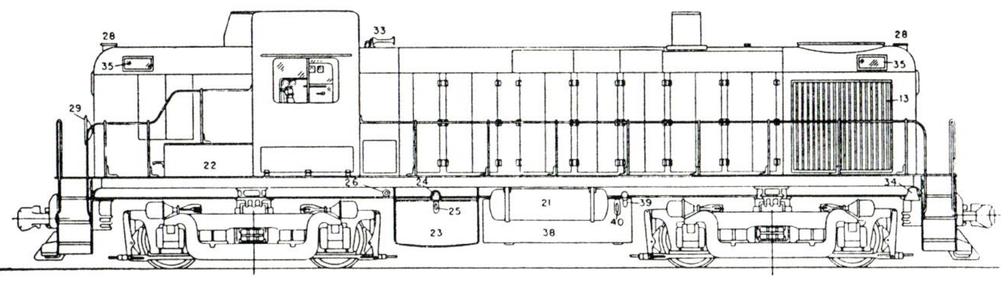

Providence, R.I.

Capitol of the smallest State, Providence was established by Roger Williams in 1636. The city was first populated by outcasts from Massachusetts. The first railroad to operate service into Providence was the Boston and Providence in 1835. Providence was also the home of Rhode Island Locomotive Works, which constructed over 2,200 steam locomotives.

Providence had a population of about 250,000 in 1950, when it was the hub of all New Haven branchlines in Rhode Island. East through the tunnel, trains ran to East Providence, Warren and Bristol, R.I. To the north over the former Providence and Worcester Railroad, trains ran to Woonsocket, R.I. and Worcester, Mass. To the west, the Pascoag Branch and the line to Willimantic, Conn. were quiet and to the south, the Pontiac Branch was a little more active. Almost every hour, local passenger service was offered to Boston as well as a few trains to Worcester, Mass. All of this, plus the Shore Line runs made Providence a very nice place to photograph New Haven Railroad equipment.

(Above) With the selection of motive power and equipment offered by the New Haven at that time, Charles Street enginehouse was the showroom of various paint combinations and locomotive models. Everything from cabs to road switchers to RDC's were recorded on color film in November 1957. *(Opposite page, top)* Charles Street roundhouse was home base for most of the original ten H-16-44's delivered to the New Haven in 1950. #597 was in its second paint scheme in August 1958, sporting the classic Loewy line of rounded windows, sloped front, and rounded headlight mounts. These H-16-44's were delivered in the fall of 1950, a few months after FM had raised the horsepower to 1600 for its hood units but before the switch to C-liner trucks. *(Opposite page, bottom)* Three GP9's led a freight under Charles Street on their way to Cedar Hill, a suburb of New Haven, in September 1957. EMD locomotives were not on the New Haven motive power roster until the mid fifties with the delivery of GP9's and twenty 1200hp yard units. These GP9's were equipped for both freight and passenger service.

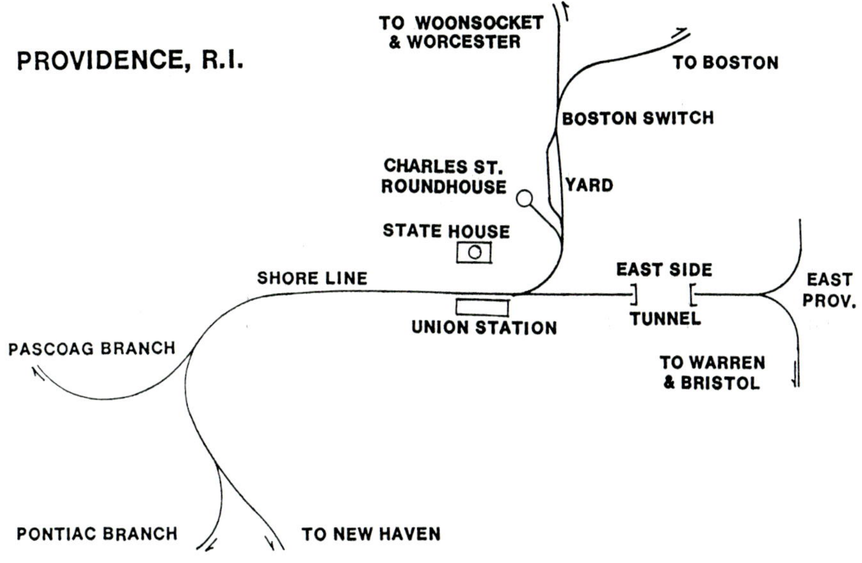

PROVIDENCE, R.I.
TO WOONSOCKET
& WORCESTER
TO BOSTON
BOSTON SWITCH
CHARLES ST.
ROUNDHOUSE
YARD
STATE HOUSE
SHORE LINE
EAST SIDE
EAST
PROV.
UNION STATION
TUNNEL
PASCOAG BRANCH
TO WARREN
& BRISTOL
PONTIAC BRANCH
TO NEW HAVEN

(Above) The date was July 1958 and #0668 in orange and black paint handled a local at the south end of Northrup Avenue yard in Providence. For local passenger and freight assignments, twelve RS1's were purchased. *(Below)* If you put a McGinnis black paint job on #598 it looked like an entirely different class of unit in this November 1957 scene. These units were originally delivered numbered in the 560s but had to be moved to the 590s to make room for the expanding fleet of RS3's.

After the flood damage of Hurricane Carol in 1954, the New Haven was very short of motive power. The US Government helped with the loan of some MRS-1's. In November 1954, a multigauge #2096 *(right)* was switching Providence yard the same as it was designed to do for the US Army in South Korea. Under the hood was an Alco 244 diesel engine just the same as in the New Haven's RS3's.

(Below) The DL109 most depicted the New Haven. With eventually 60 units in the class, these cab units ran up and down the relatively level Shore Line in pairs on passenger and freight assignments and later singly on passenger locals. The DL109's had a pair of 539 diesel engines rated at 1000hp each. They became the backbone of the fleet during WWII. #0718 was built in January 1943 and retired in the 3rd quarter of 1957 about one year after this July 1956 photograph.

#930 *(above)* was a high hood 660hp switch engine. A loyal Alco customer, the New Haven had purchased the first HH600 back in 1931 and continued to purchase them through 1940. #0930, the last built of the New England high hood units, was built in February of 1940 just in time to handle the wartime traffic. Most of its career was devoted to shunting cars at South Boston, but late in its life worked assignments at Providence. Using the old arrangement of chains to keep the Blunt trucks under the unit in case of a derailment, #0930 handled the light switching operation of Providence during September of 1957. *(Below)* After purchasing the C-line demonstrators, the New Haven took delivery of eight more 2400hp *Consolidation Line* passenger A units. New Haven was the third railroad to order this model unit from Fairbanks Morse. #796 was one of the three C-liners never repainted into McGinnis colors. New Haven owned almost all of the New England railroads' FM's, thirty-seven out of the thirty- nine units.   *(bottom-Ralph Phillips photo collection of DRS)*

(Above) Three RS11's headed for Providence with a Shore Line train holding down the advertised schedule. Attleboro, Massachusetts was the location of this March 1957 photograph, just east of the Rhode Island line. Fifteen RS11's were purchased in 1956 to replace the aging fleet of DL109's, along with thirty GP9's and fifteen H-16-44's. Numbered 1400 to 1414, these units handled passenger runs for about three years and lasted right up to the beginning of Conrail in freight service. *(Below)* S1 #995 performed switching duties at Attleboro in September 1957 before taking the local freight to Providence. The red cab with black hood was one of many McGinnis color schemes applied to the switcher roster. New Haven's fleet of sixty-five S1's were purchased over a period of time from 1941 to 1949. #995 was the very last S1 delivered to the New Haven in January 1949. Very pronounced from this view was the altered roof contour on the cab of this Alco switcher.

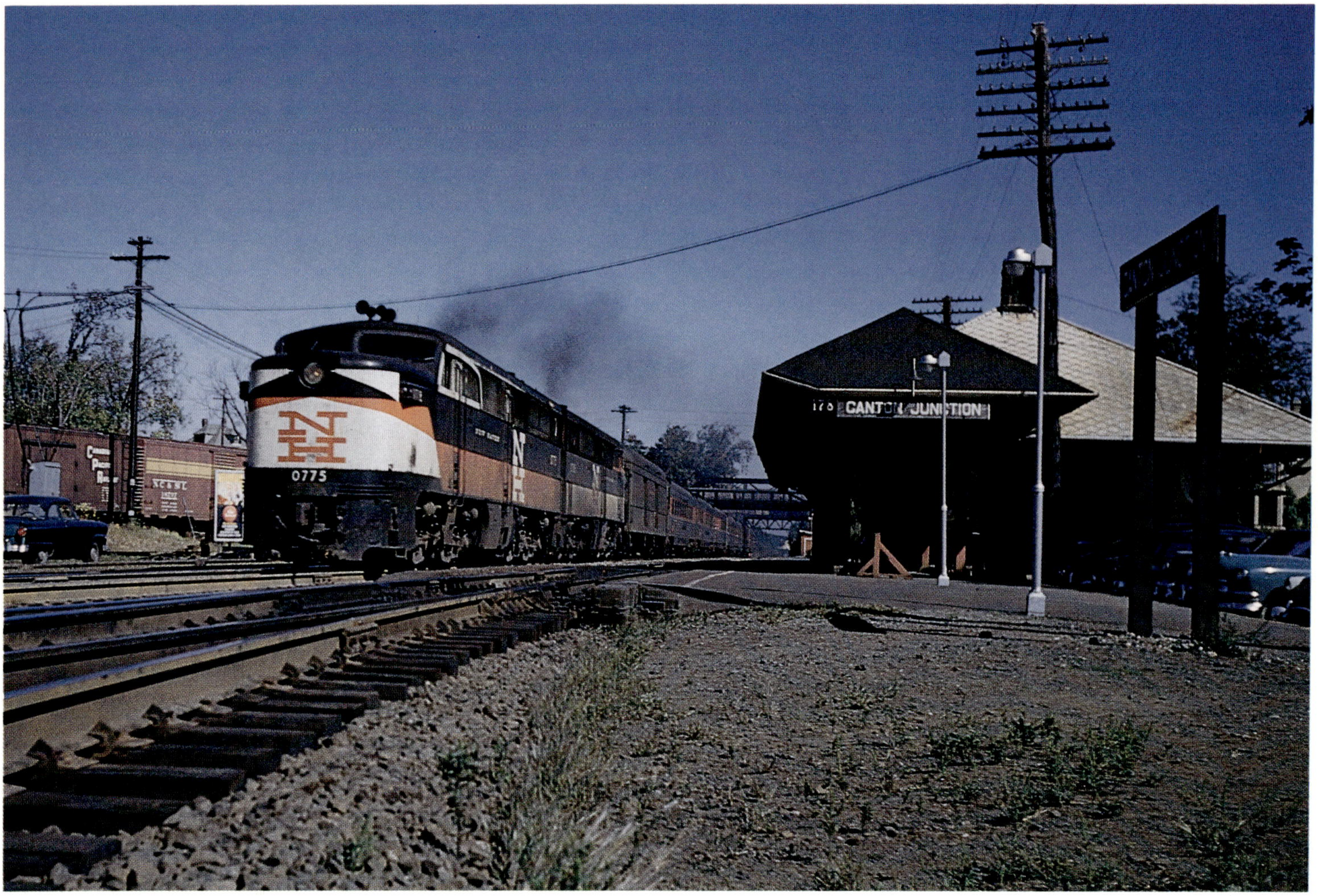

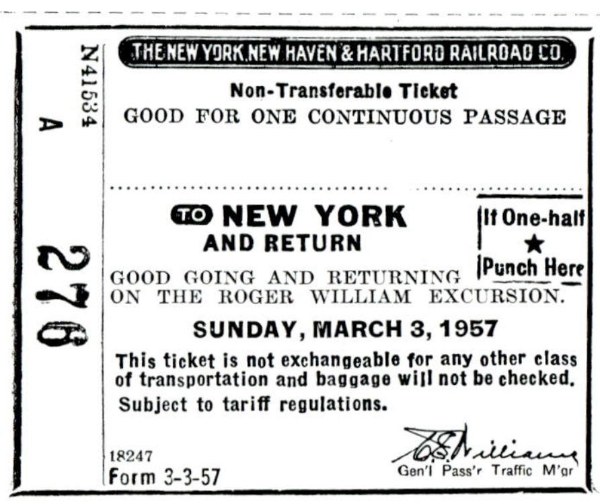

(Above) At track speed two PA's whisked a Washington train through Canton Junction on their way south. Boston to Providence was 44 miles in 44 minutes including Back Bay or Route 128 station stops, taxing the capacity of the 16 cylinder 244's to quickly accelerate the train from station stops or speed restrictions. #0775 with lower red panels in the McGinnis color scheme was followed by the second PA with white lower panels in this September 1957 scene.

(Opposite page) Leaving Rhode Island for Boston, an A-B-A set of FA's accelerated a freight train just north of Boston Switch. #0423 was very clean in the new green and yellow colors in this February 1955 scene. From this higher view point, the yellow nose stripe over the headlight was clearly visible. The FA1 plus FB1 plus FA1 combination was set up just the way they were ordered and delivered from Alco in 1947.

N41534
A
276

THE NEW YORK NEW HAVEN & HARTFORD RAILROAD CO.

Non-Transferable Ticket

GOOD FOR ONE CONTINUOUS PASSAGE

TO NEW YORK AND RETURN

If One-half ★ Punch Here

GOOD GOING AND RETURNING ON THE ROGER WILLIAM EXCURSION.

SUNDAY, MARCH 3, 1957

This ticket is not exchangeable for any other class of transportation and baggage will not be checked. Subject to tariff regulations.

18247
Form 3-3-57

Gen'l Pass'r Traffic M'gr

THE PULLMAN COMPANY—Passenger's Check. To identify accommodations purchased.

Providence to Washington, D. C.

SEAT	CAR	DATE
9		19

Property taken into car will be entirely at owner's risk

OFFICE 5-6 FORM 15

1065

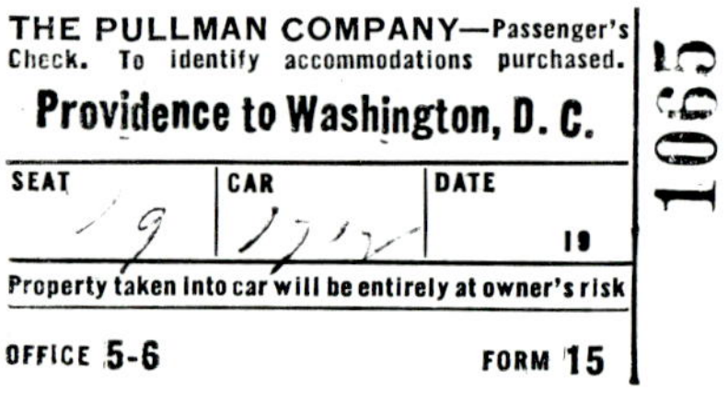

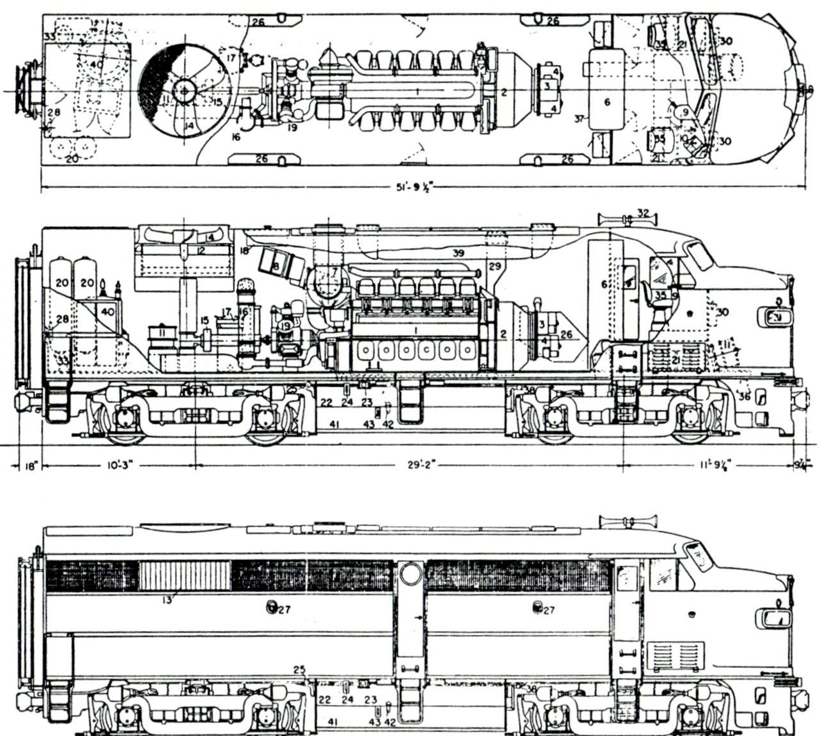

NEW HAVEN
COTTON

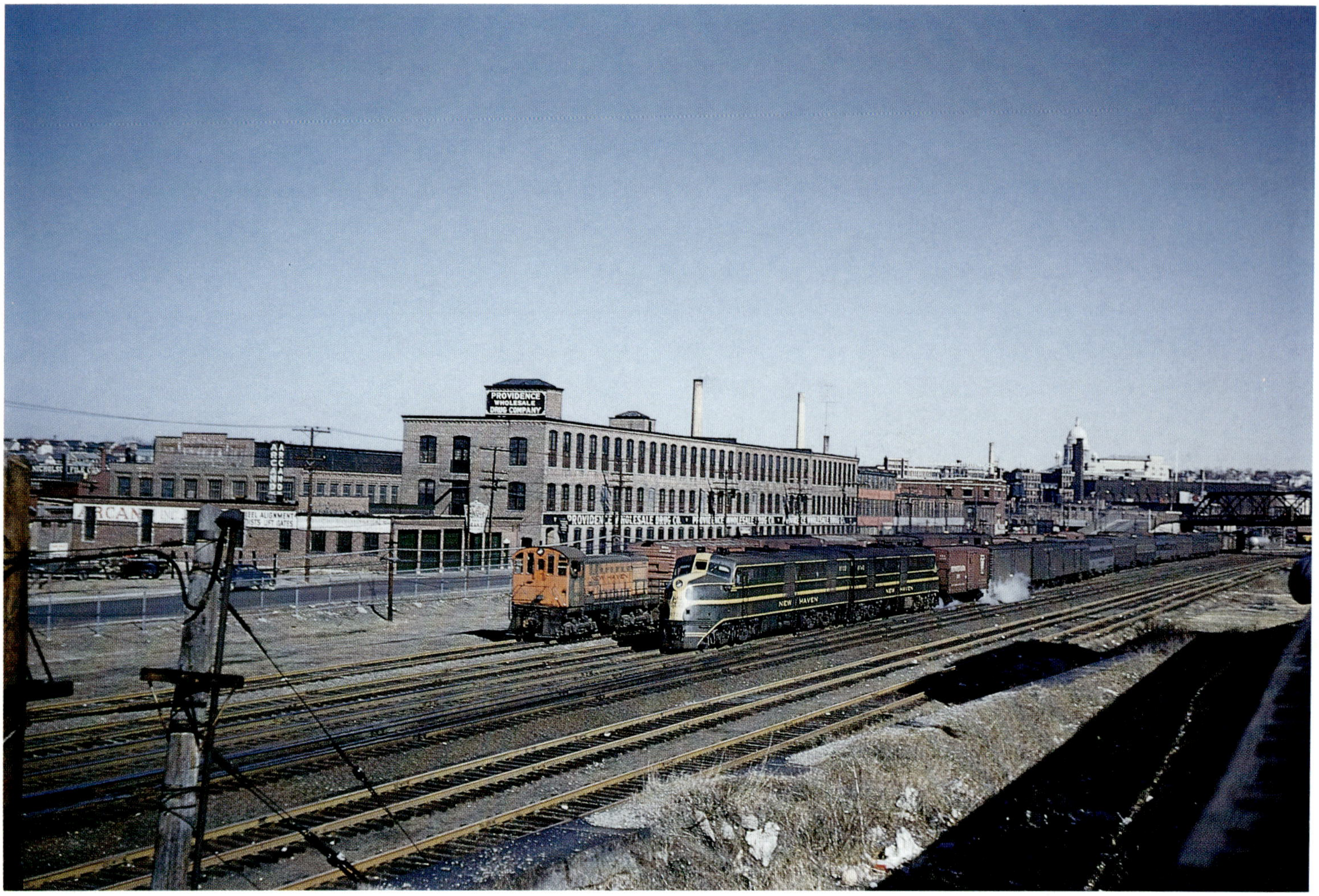

(Above) Still covering mainline assignments in February 1955, two DL109's accelerated a Shore Line train out of Union Station in Providence. With the dome of the State Capitol visible over the train, the 0700's passed an S1 switching the produce yard. Replacement power was delivered by the summer of 1956 and the 0700's were transferred to local passenger runs out of Boston.

(Opposite page) On June 10, 1955, two PA's stopped at Providence on their way south. The signal line whistled two blasts and the engineer notched out the throttle to move fourteen cars to New London. Only three PA's received the original McGinnis paint scheme with white on the lower panels. White turned out to be too difficult to keep clean, so the red and white bands switched places on the remaining engines so painted.

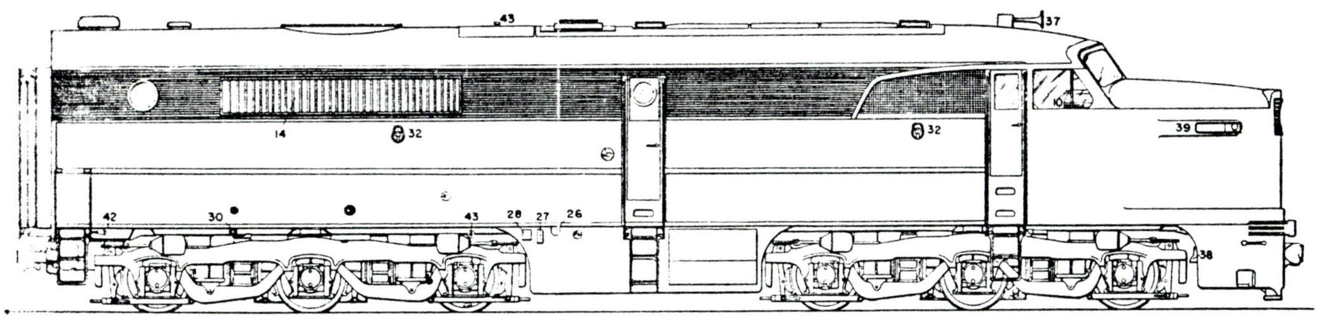

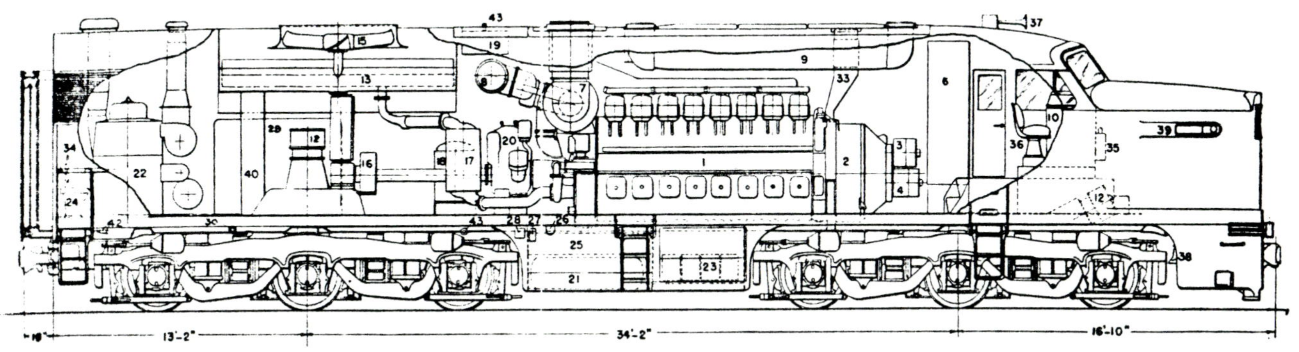
13-2"   34-2"   16-10"

Woonsocket, R.I.

Back in the early fifties, New Haven's President Dumaine had an idea that branchline passenger costs could be reduced with the operation of a rail bus. In 1951, Mack built the first FCD car for the New Haven. FCD stood for Frederick C. Dumaine. The six cylinder 200hp diesel powered four GE traction motors on trucks similar to a PCC. With seating for 45, it could easily handle the Providence to Worcester run. Photographed *(below)* at Woonsocket, R.I. on July 21, 1954, #10 was followed by an order for 9 more, but slightly different FCD Type II units equipped for MU operation. #10 was soon replaced by #12 on the "Little Shore Line" assignment between Worcester and Providence. Only #10 and #12 were used in revenue service, all the rest just sat at Readville waiting for resale.

Myricks, Mass.

(Opposite page) In June 1845, the Fall River Branch was opened from Myricks, Mass. on the Boston to New Bedford Line, to Central Street, Fall River, 10.8 miles. In this September 1958 scene at Myricks, RS2 #0505 with a load of US Army tank cars entered the New Bedford line. The 244 diesel started to accelerate the local through the switches as the fireman hooped up the orders on the head end and the conductor did the same from the NE5 caboose at the rear. The orders indicated a meet with RDC #24 at Taunton. Later RDC-1 #24 roared past, running a little late on its way to Fall River.

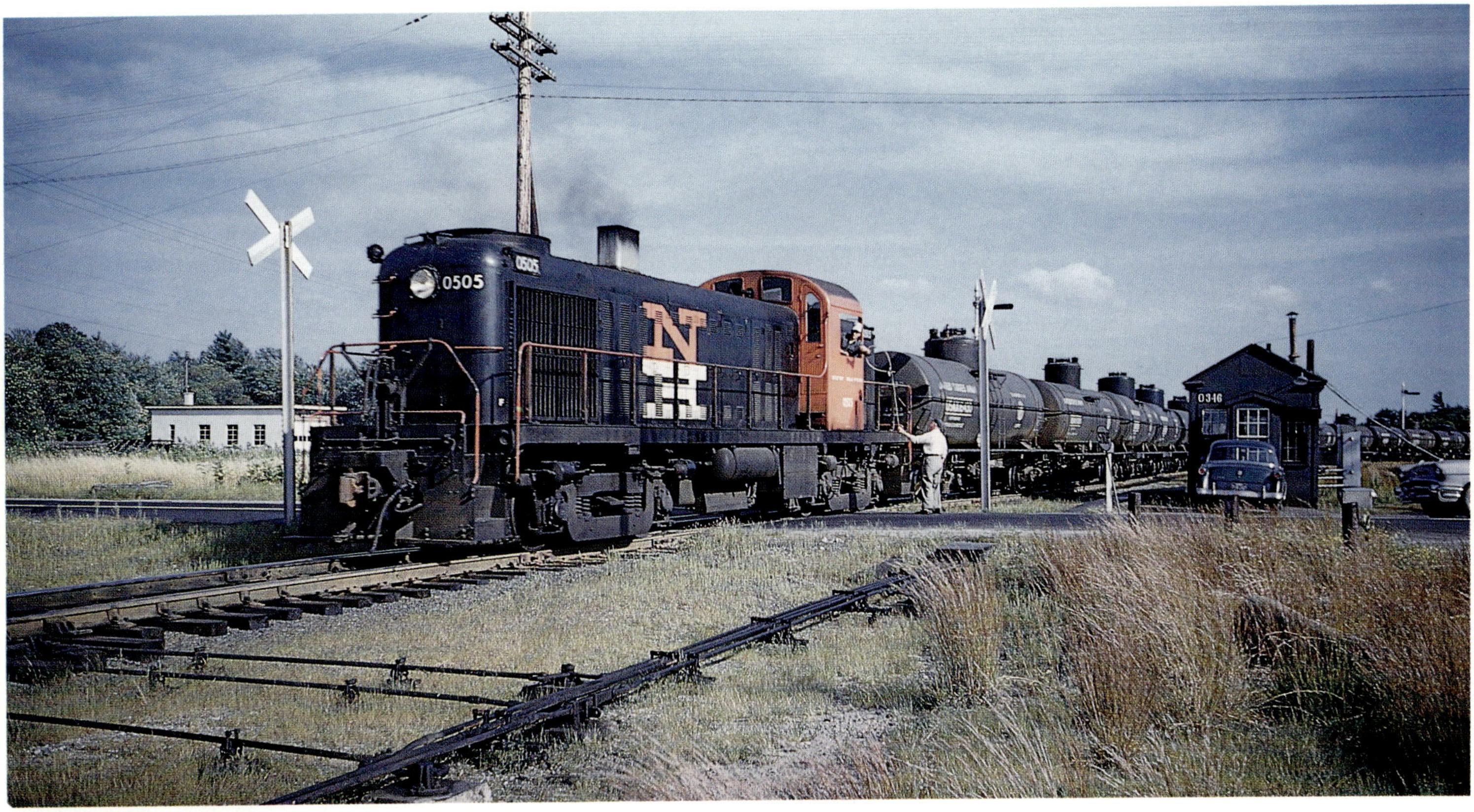

The New York New Haven and Hartford RAILROAD CO.

Budd

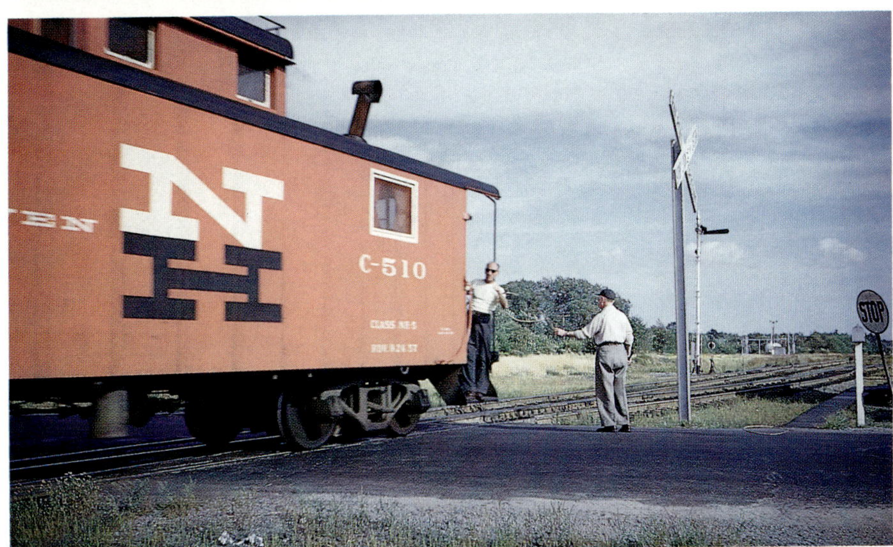

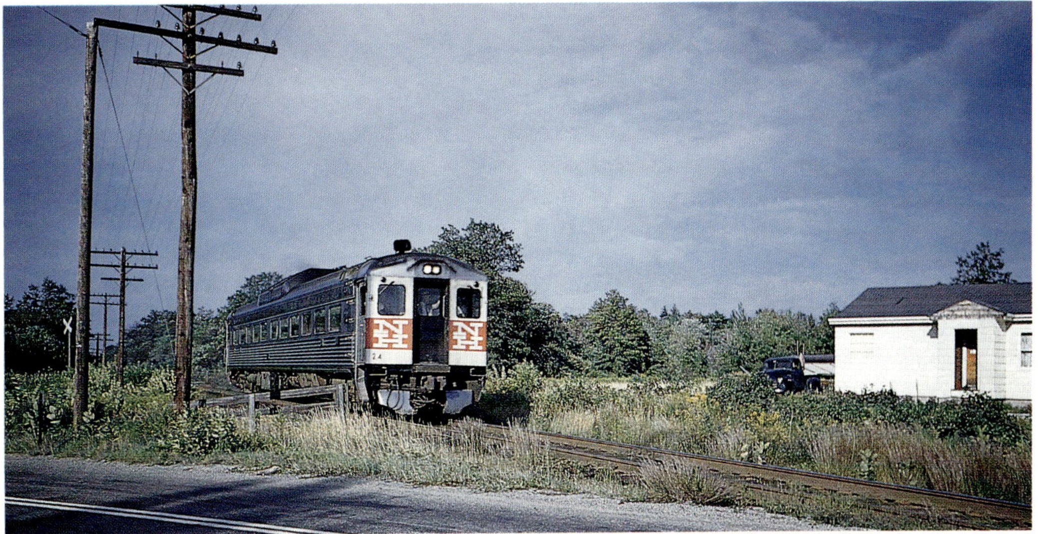

Buzzards Bay, Mass.

Buzzards Bay, Massachusetts was the location where the railroad crossed the Cape Cod Canal and the hub of the New Haven's Cape operation. During the summer months, the station was particularly busy with people from Boston and New York City wanting relief from the hot cities.

(Above) It was mid-morning in June 1956 as RS2 #0509 brought in the Woods Hole section of the New York train. *(Opposite page, top)* A few minutes later PA1 #0783 crossed the vertical lift bridge and arrived with the Hyannis section where the two sections were combined for the trip to New York. *(Opposite page, bottom)* Just before departure the RDC's cleared the block and arrived with the Cape train from South Station, Boston.

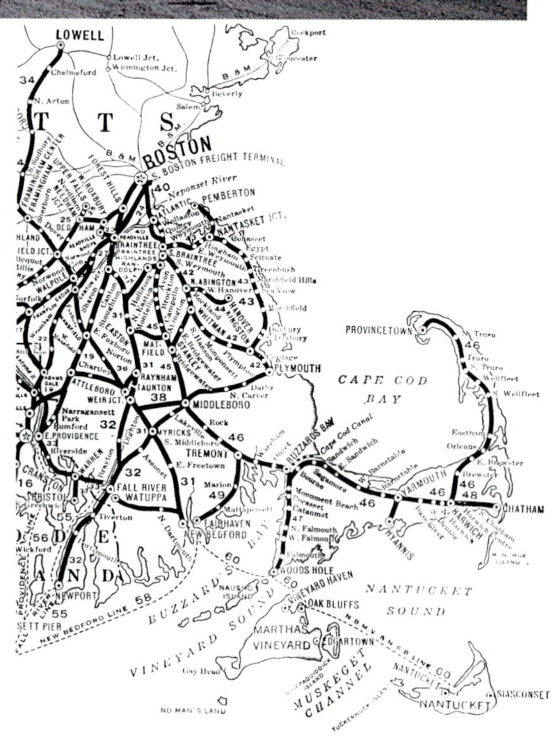

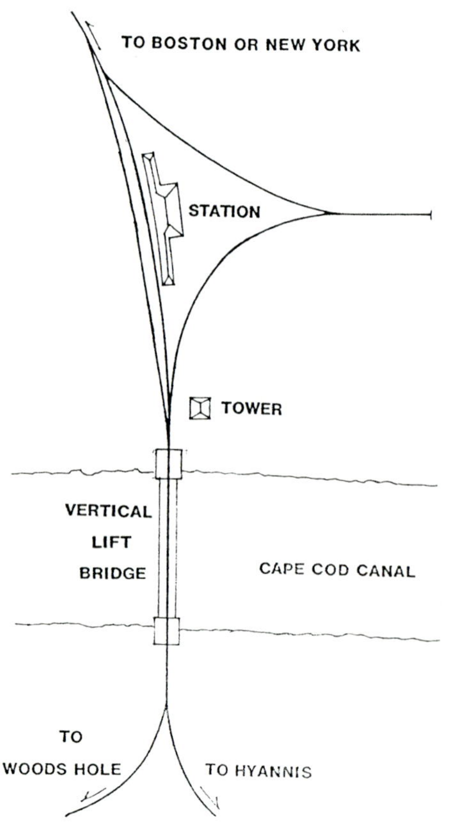

The eight mile Cape Cod Canal was completed in 1914 requiring the building of the large vertical lift bridge for the New Haven to cross the canal. On the east end of the canal bridge, the tracks divided with RDC #22 *(top)* swinging to the left for Wood Hole and the boat connections to the islands.

(Opposite page, top) Minutes later, RDC #23 turned to the right for service to Hyannis, the largest town on the Cape. These RDC-1's had split at Buzzards Bay station before crossing the bridge separately.

(Opposite page, bottom) Heading the train from Boston was NH #137, a rare RDC-4 handling US Mail for Buzzards Bay and the Cape. New Haven owned three RDC-4's, #135-137, built by the Budd Company in 1953 and used almost exclusively in Boston-Cape Cod service.

NEW HAVEN

Boston, Mass.

Boston, Massachusetts was the "Hub City" for the B&M. Its President George Hannauer announced plans for a new North Station in 1927. The station would have a sports arena and hotel along Causeway Street in Boston with elevated trolley tracks over the street leading to the station. The waiting room and station were opened in 1928, part of the B&M modernization program. Twenty two stub-end tracks faced the Boston Garden and North Station waiting room to handle the passenger traffic at B&M's most active station. Four new drawbridges were completed over the Charles River in 1930 furnishing eight tracks to the entrance of the station. It was this area that was the focal point of this color photography from 1953 through 1958.

(Opposite page, top) Most of the B&M 244 powered Alcos were RS3's. #1517 had just been delivered in October 1954, when it was assigned to commuter service, passing SW9 #1230 on its way into North Station. #1517 was the last unit delivered from the 1954 Alco order, which placed another 4-6-2 into retirement. By the mid 1950's, silver trucks were added to the classic B&M color scheme. *(Opposite page, bottom)* RS3 #1513 showed the newer paint scheme with the *Minute Man* on the cab side as it left North Station during the evening commuter rush of June 1955. The major 1955 order for 55 RDC's was starting to be delivered. Within a few years these RS3's would move to freight service. *(This page, above)* RS3 #1543, an RS3 without the *Minute Man* on the cab, teamed with sister #1545 to handle a milk train. In September 1958, RS3's in passenger service and on milk trains were beginning to be a rare scene at North Station. *(This page, below)* But not all B&M Alco road switchers were delivered in red, the original RS2 #1500 was painted in the black switcher scheme when it was delivered in May of 1948. Sporting white flags, #1500 was working the Boston area in September 1958. This unit was formerly Alco RS2 demonstrator #1500. *(Photos, this page- Ralph Phillips, DRS Collection)*

(Above) B&M Alco S5 #864 switched the Charlestown yard in July of 1954, one month after delivery. One of a group of six units, these 800hp S5's were the only 251 powered Alcos on the system and the only 251 powered switchers on a New England roster. Numbered #860 to #865, the S5's worked the Boston area and several were later upgraded to 1000hp.

(Opposite page, top) Even in 1955, the original FLYING YANKEE called on Boston daily. After discharging its passengers, the train backed out of the station and turned on the wye before returning north. Built in February 1935, the B&M/MEC train originally operated on a Boston to Bangor, Maine schedule. #6000 was similiar to the PIONEER ZEPHYR, but without a baggage and mail compartment. The Budd built equipment seated 142 in a three car train. Over the years, it was also assigned to Boston to White River Jct. and Boston to Troy, N.Y. runs.

(Opposite page, bottom) #1495 waited beside its replacement at the East Somerville enginehouse at Boston. The one hundred plus B-15 moguls were the workhorses of the B&M, handling both passenger and freight assignments. Having just completed her commuter run on the Clinton Branch in December 1955, she was serviced for the evening run. These 2-6-0's worked the entire system before their final duties in Boston.

FLYING YANKEE

1495
BOSTON AND MAINE

(Above) It was June 1953 at North Station Boston, when #3807 led a long excursion train of "American Flyer" lightweight coaches. E7 #3807 was actually carrying a new E8 cab after a wreck in 1949 and rebuilt by EMD in 1950. The skyline of North Station was about to change with the new expressway starting to cover the hotel and the Boston Garden and the railroad scene was about to change with the delivery of the RDC's. *(Opposite page)* In January 1958, Fairbanks Morse delivered two P-12-42's to power the B&M's new *Talgo* train. Originally designed for the Boston- Portland inter-city run, the *Talgo* train spent most of its active years in commuter service around Boston. Numbered #1 and #2, the B&M units had a 1600hp opposed-piston diesel engine, 1200hp for traction and 400hp for head end power, placed in a low-slung carbody. Photographed in March 1958, the unit had one of the famous McGinnis color schemes. These were the only FM units on the B&M system.

(Opposite page- Ralph Phillips photo, DRS Collection)

(Above) Just after World War II, the B&M ordered three A-B sets of F2's for passenger service for the lower speed operation in the hilly territory. At the diesel shop in October 1958, idled #4226 A&B now painted in one of the experimental McGinnis paint schemes. This F2 set lasted another eight years before retirement in 1966. The B&M rostered twenty-one of the seventy-six F2's built for the US roads. The passenger F2's were numbered 4224 A&B to 4226 A&B and the freight F2's #4250-#4264. *(Opposite page)* After a roundhouse fire at Springfield, Mass., a 660hp S3 unit #1174 was rebuilt by Alco in November 1957 to a 1000hp S4. This was the first Alco switcher painted in blue, and the last one delivered by Alco to the B&M. In September 1958, #1274 was handling one of the many Boston switching assignments. It used the heavier weight and higher horsepower to start and move larger cuts. Boston and Maine's group of S4's were numbered #1266 to #1273. *(Both, Ralph Phillips photos, DRS Collection)*

BOSTON and MAINE
RAILROAD
"MINUTE MAN SERVICE"

(Above) On June 30, 1954, #3709 took a spin at Boston. This 4-6-2 was the last of ten P-3a Pacifics, built by Alco in 1923 for the B&M. #3700 to 3709 often carried the GREEN MOUNTAIN FLYER to Bellows Falls or Rutland, Vermont in better years. As the last active member of her class, this Pacific was now relegated to Boston to Lowell local service and would be active for only one more year. In the background, the roundhouse was now filled with diesel units instead of steam power. *(Below)* Geeps were used in commuter service along with the BL2's and RS3's, but this GP7 was a little different. It was not one of the B&M 1500's, but the Portland Terminal #1081 dressed and painted just like its big brothers from the B&M. Built in December, 1950, PT #1081 ran off mileage on the B&M until sold to the MEC in 1956 and renumbered #581. In this June 1955 photograph, #1081 was still a non-MU passenger Geep handling a train to Reading, Mass.

(Above) The B&M started dieselization of road freight service with eight A-B sets of FT's in 1943 and early 1944. More FT's were delivered in the fall of 1944 to surplus most B&M 2-8-4's. Now at the end of their career, 4210A and B waited outside the diesel shop. Photographed on August 24, 1957 just a few days before this A-B set was returned to La Grange, Ill. for trade in on new GP9's.

(Bottom) Not all switching power was in the 600 to 1200hp range. In November of 1940, the B&M received four 380hp GE 44 tonners, several working the Boston area on lighter assignments saving the cost of a fireman under the 1937 90,000# one man locomotive agreement. B&M eventually had ten 44 tonners on its roster. One year after this October 1958 picture, #112 was sold to the Hoosac Tunnel and Wilmington, better known as the "Hoot, Toot and Whistle."

(Both- Ralph Phillips Photos, DRS Collection)

THE CHURCH
CANADIAN NATIONAL
CNR
1806
1803
1802

PORTLAN
CANADIAN NATIONAL
GRAND TRUNK
4446
4446
4450

Portland, Me.

Portland is the largest city in the State of Maine and the chief seaport. Settled in 1632, Portland is located on Casco Bay which leads to the Atlantic Ocean. It was also the junction of the Maine Central, Boston & Maine and the Grand Trunk Railroads. The Portland Terminal Company interconnected these railroads and handled most of the switching of the docks. In April of 1956, PT #1001, a high hood 600hp Alco, was still switching the depot. Built in 1937, it was the senior member of the PT diesel fleet and was photographed *(above)* beside the high ball signal at Portland station.

(Opposite page, top) One month before, Canadian National RS3's #1803 and #1806 were laying over in the Grand Trunk yard after a snow covered run from Montreal. Until becoming completely dieselized later in the year, the Grand Trunk used CN RS3's on the through runs to and from Canada. #1803 was built in November 1954, part of the first group of five CN RS3's. Two months after this photo they were renumbered in the 3000s.

(Opposite page, bottom) Three years later in February of 1959, the GP9's still looked as if they had just been delivered from EMD. The units were lettered "Grand Trunk" not "Grand Trunk Western." 4446 and 4450 were part of the freight group delivered with dynamic brakes. Geeps lettered "Grand Trunk" were #4442 to #4450, #4902 to #4906, and #4558 and #4559.

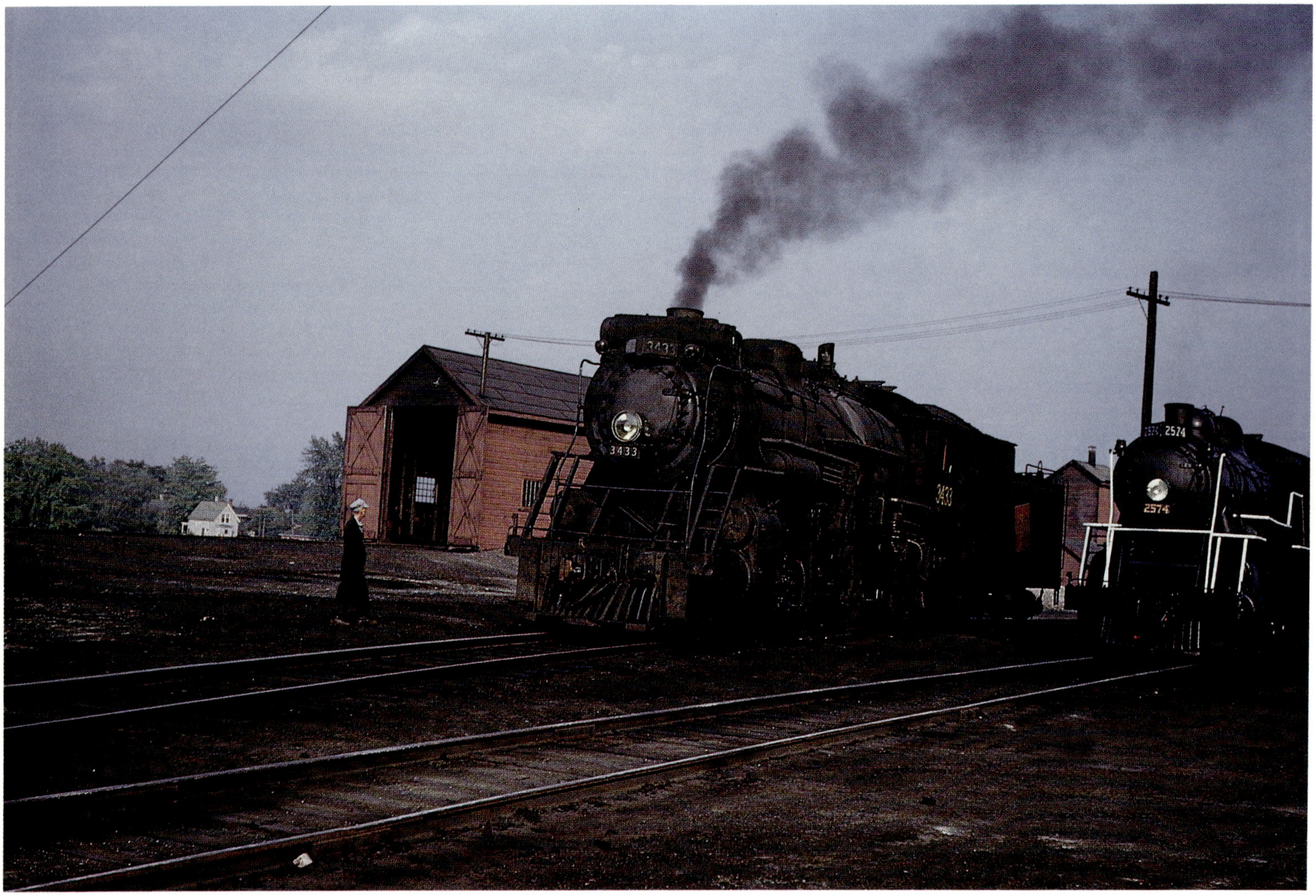

The Grand Trunk steam power was actually serviced north of the city at East Deering. Back in June of 1953, the GT assembled six steamers to double head on three sections of the Ringling Brothers, Barnum and Bailey circus trains. Part of this team was #3433 *(above)*, a 2-8-2 built by Baldwin in 1913, #3704 *(opposite page, top)* a USRA 2-8-2 built by Alco in 1918, and #2574 *(opposite page, bottom)*, a 1907 Alco 2-8-0. #2574 was the last GT steam locomotive in New England, held at Island Pond, Vermont until September 1959.

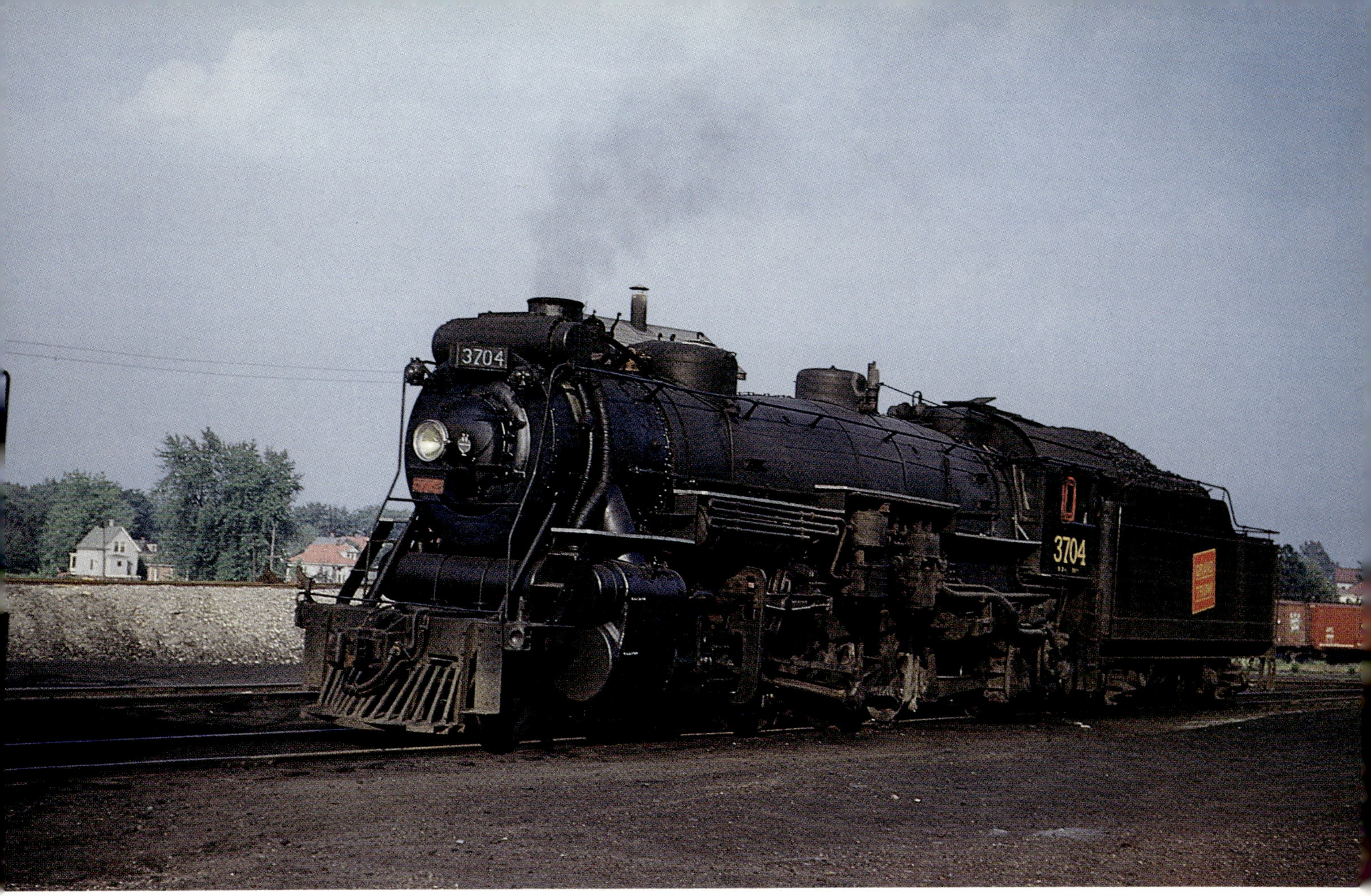
3704
3704

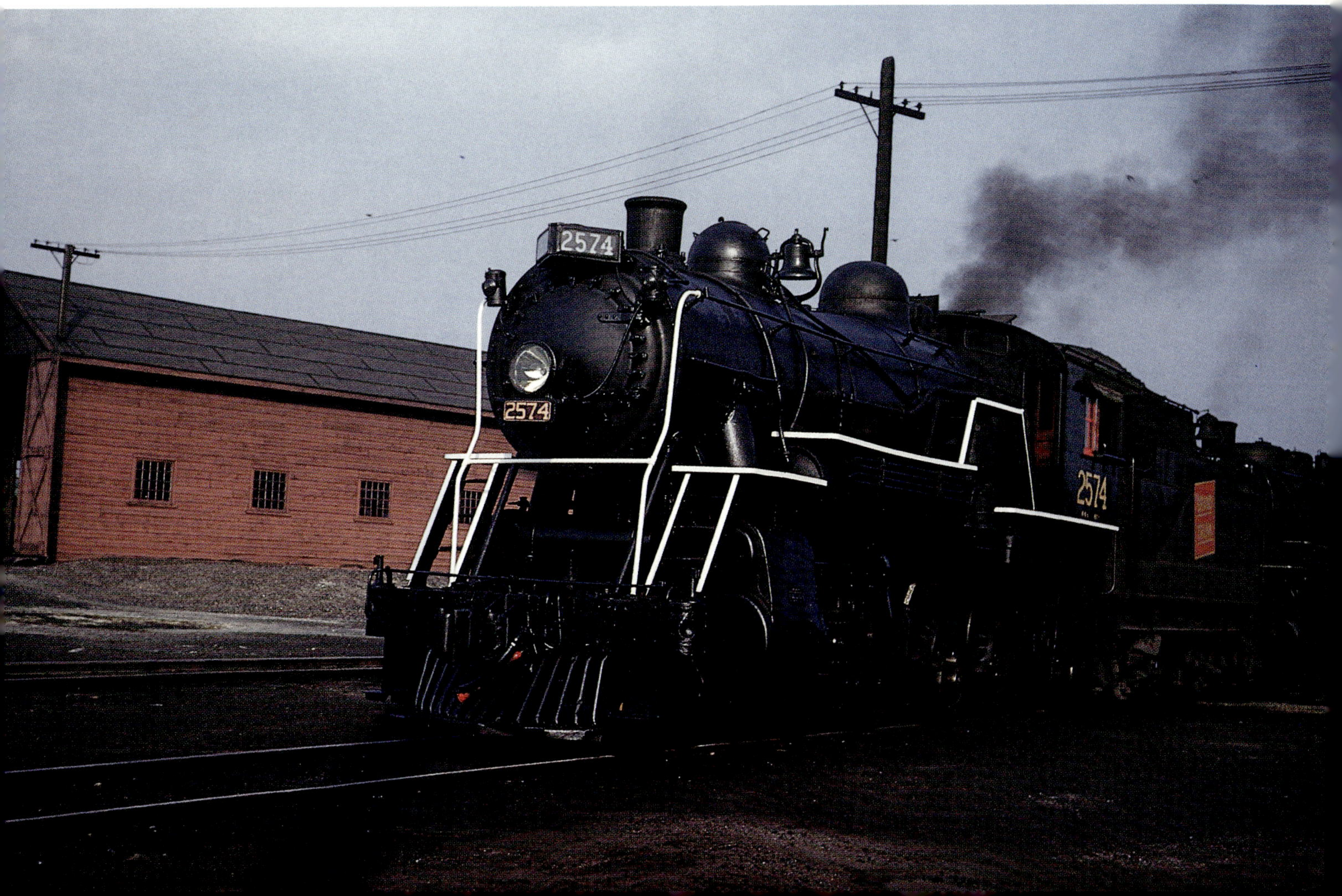
2574
2574
2574

(Above) 0-6-0 #7527 did the switching honors at Portland in March of 1956. In three months #7527 left Portland for the last time and by the end of the year all steam was gone. #7527 was the first of five 0-6-0's, #7527-7531 built by Alco in 1919 for the Grand Trunk. *(Opposite page)* Later that morning, CN 4-6-2 #5280 prepared to take #17 north to Montreal. It was winter time and the consist was small, mainly mail and express business for the small towns in Maine, New Hampshire and Vermont along the route. Unfortunately, this Victorian styled station was destroyed in 1966 to avoid the city taxes.

1051
PT
1051
PORTLAND TERMINAL

802
802
MAINE CENTRAL

Back in September 1945, the B&M purchased two E7's, #3800 and 3801. Numbered to follow after the newest Pacifics, this unit led a fleet of 21 E7's. In August 1957, #3800 was still pulling the "varnish" between Boston and Portland when photographed *(above)* at the South Portland enginehouse. #3800 was equipped with small number boards until its retirement in 1959.

Just before World War II, the Portland Terminal Company purchased one Alco S2 switcher numbered #1051, the first 1000hp unit on the roster. It was a good purchase for the PT, because the unit ran 40 years before being retired in 1981. Pictured working the Portland station *(opposite page, top)* in February 1959, #1051 passed the street at the north end of the station while making up a train for Boston. The whine of the turbo was just audible over the clanking Blunt trucks as she crossed the street.

In 1956 the Maine Central went shopping for more units when traffic levels increased. Since EMD had a long lead time for delivery of their GP9's, Maine Central turned to Alco for two RS11's. One was delivered as #801, however the other was delivered through the subsidiary Portland Terminal as #1082. Within six months it was relettered MEC 802. #801 and #802 were considered just another Geep in the road pool. #802 was photographed *(opposite page, bottom)* at Portland in May of 1963 awaiting her next road assignment.

Yarmouth Jct., Me.

Yarmouth Junction, located 12 miles north of the Portland GT station, was where the Grand Trunk crossed the Brunswick main of the Maine Central. *(Top)* On June 24, 1954, 2-8-2 #3716 carried the GT wayfreight south to Portland. Having started earlier in the day at Gorham, N.H., the local crossed the diamond and headed for the Portland enginehouse at East Deering to be serviced for the return trip in the morning. #3716 was the last of seventeen USRA light 2-8-2's built by Alco in 1918, some were later transferred to the CN. Three years later almost to the day on June 28, 1957, the #3716 made her last trip over the GT, ignominiously hauled dead from Island Pond, Vermont to Montreal.

(Opposite page, top) GP7 #581 stopped momentarily in August 1957 to pick up passengers on its southbound trip from Rockland to Portland. With a New Haven baggage car and sleeper in the train, the final destination would be New York City. Passenger service to Rockland continued until April 1959. The non-MU MEC Geep was formerly Portland Terminal #1081 and was transferred to the MEC in 1956 to be later equipped with MU.

(Opposite page, bottom)) Grand Trunk #16 stopped a little later the same day on its way to Portland. It was summertime and a lot of Canadians were on their way south to the Maine beaches. #4902 was the first of five GP9's delivered one year earlier to the Grand Trunk to dieselize their passenger operation. This train continued to operate on a daily-except-Sunday basis through the summer of 1960. In 1957, the year of this photograph, over 25,000 passengers rode trains #16 and #17 between Island Pond, Vermont and Portland, Maine.

YARMOUTH JUNCTION
581
V
236

4902
GRAND TRUNK
YARMOUTH JUNCTION

Danville Jct., Me.

Twenty seven miles north of Portland, west by railroad direction, the Grand Trunk crossed the inland main of the Maine Central at Danville Jct. On July 24, 1954, mixed train #189 *(above)* waited for #17 to make its connecting run to Lewiston, Maine. Since the Grand Trunk line missed the cities of Lewiston and Auburn, seven miles north of Danville Jct., a branch was built 5.4 miles to connect with these cities and then leased to the GT. #189 ran this route *(opposite page)* daily-except- Sunday 24 minutes after the departure of #17. The old wooden Canadian National combine handled all mail, baggage and passengers for the short run to Lewiston. Power for this run was Grand Trunk #3410, a class S-1-f 2-8-2 built by Alco in 1913. Its 51,000 pounds of tractive effort were more than adequate for the assignment. #3410 continued to provide service right up to dieselization.

Burnham Jct., Me.

On the mainline between Waterville and Bangor, the Maine Central passed through the small community of Burnham Jct. This junction connected the MEC and the Belfast & Moosehead Lake. In 1869, the short line reached the junction but never made it to Moosehead Lake in Northern Maine. The railroad was built to bring lumber and farm products to Belfast, Maine for shipping down the coast. From 1871 to 1925 the line was leased to the MEC by the City of Belfast who later operated it themselves.

(Above) Even in August of 1958, the B&ML still offered connecting passenger and mail service. With a wooden mail car and coach, GE 70 tonner #50 waited patiently for the Maine Central passenger train to arrive. This picture was out of the twenties, but without steam power.

(Opposite page, top) Another one of the three locomotives, #51 provided the motive power for the freight cars being interchanged between roads in September 1958. The two 70 tonners delivered in November 1946 were supplemented by #52 in 1951 to dieselize the line.

(Opposite page, bottom) On the same day, MEC #708 made a momentary stop for two passengers and two mail sacks at Burnham Jct. Approaching the station, the E7 was one of four purchased in 1946 with Rock Island maroon and silver gray colors. It passed the typical MEC wig-wag crossing protection before stopping at the station.

BELFAST AND MOOSEHEAD LAKE RAILROAD	NOT GOOD AFTER DATE PUNCHED		
ROUND TRIP	DAY	1	Jan Feb
CASH FARE RECEIPT	2	3	Mar Apr
No. 4822	4	5	May Jun
	6	7	Jul Aug
GOOD IN COACHES ONLY	8	9	Sep Oct
FROM	10	11	Nov Dec
Belfast	12	13	NINETEEN HUNDRED
TO	14	15	TENS UNITS
Burnham	16	17	0 0
AND RETURN	18	19	1 1
This ticket is good for one Round Trip passage in coaches only within final limit punched in margin and is subject to regulations applying to Round Trip for which fare is paid.	20	21	2 2
	22	23	3 3
	24	25	4 4
	26	27	5 5
	28	29	6 6
	30	31	7 7
			8 8
182237 *W.L. Brown* GENERAL MANAGER			9 9

	AMOUNT COLLECTED		
	$	¢	¢
	1	10	1
ONE DAY RT	2	20	2
★ 30 DAY RT	3	30	3
★ SPECIAL	4	40	4
★ TAX EXEMPT	5	50	5
PASSAGE CANCELLATIONS BELOW	6	60	6
GOING RETURN	7	70	7
	8	80	8
	9	90	9

If One-half ★ Punch Here · Form C.F.4

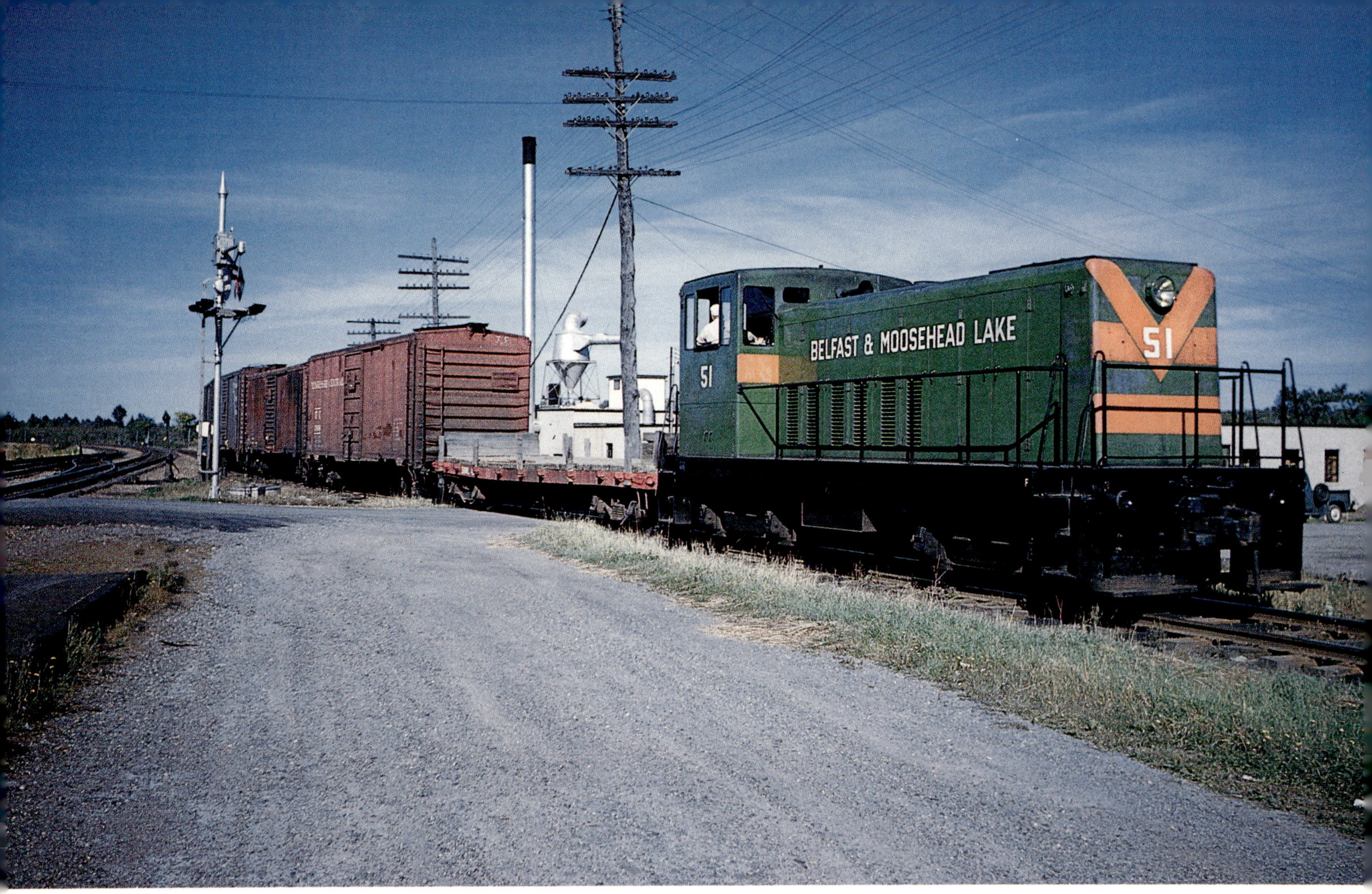

BELFAST & MOOSEHEAD LAKE
51

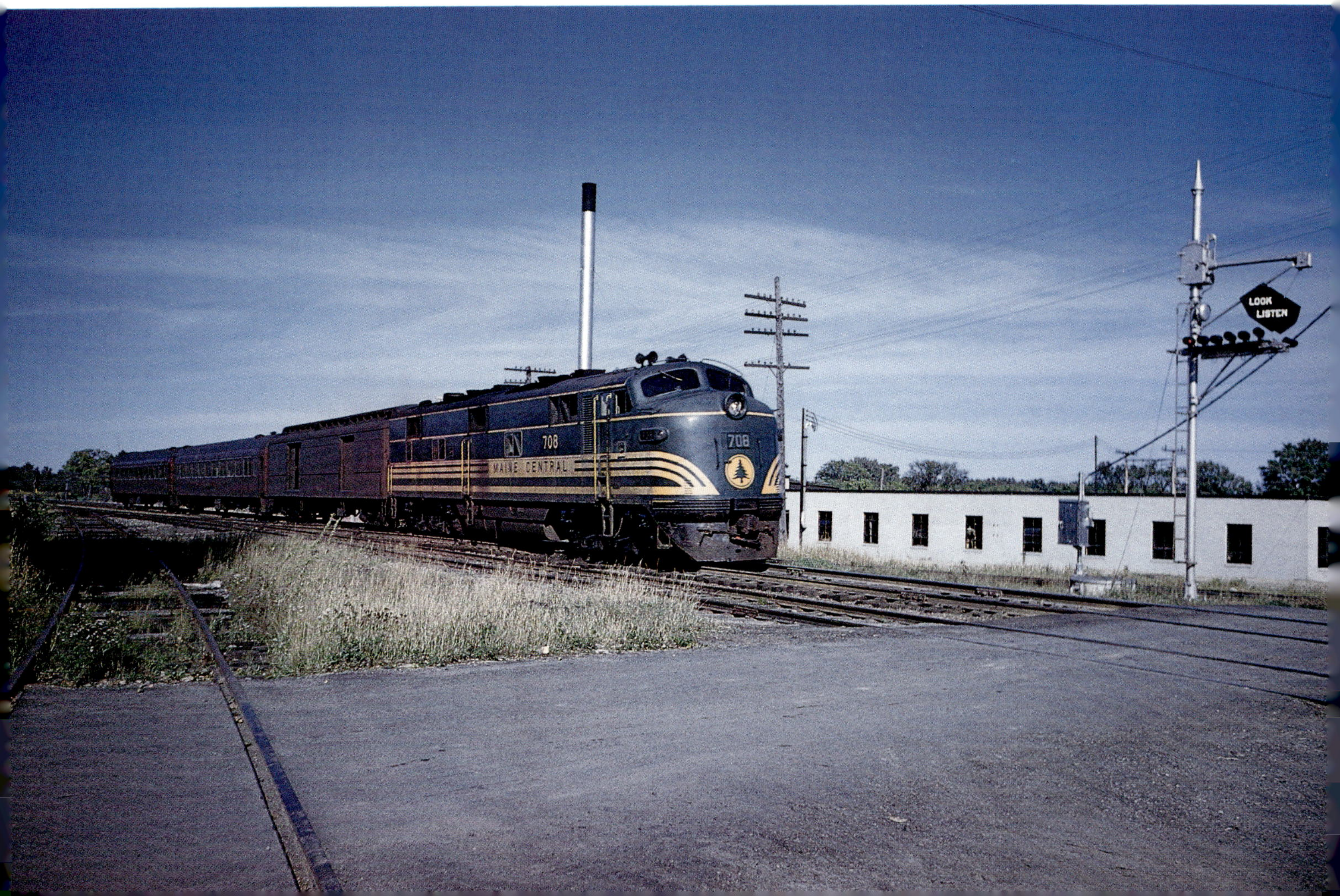

708
MAINE CENTRAL
LOOK
LISTEN

Northern Maine Jct., Me.

Six miles west of Bangor out on the plain, lies Northern Maine Jct., a major yard and enginehouse for the BAR with a connection to the MEC. In 1905 the BAR constructed a 26 mile line from South Lagrange to connect with the Maine Central and to avoid the old route which went through Old Town and Bangor. Crossing over the MEC mainline, the BAR proceeded south to the seaport of Searsport; however, most of the traffic was interchanged at Northern Maine Jct. with the MEC.

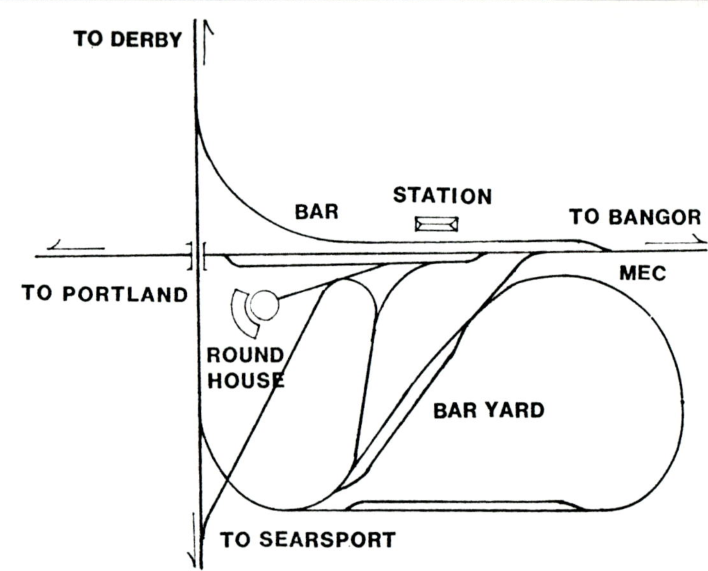

(Opposite page, top) In May of 1957, F3 #40 led a southbound freight over the MEC mainline. Coupled with a BL2 and a GP7 the consist displayed the three basic types of units used for road power. Eight F3's, eight BL2's and fifteen GP7's formed the summer road pool of engines. *(Opposite page, bottom)* BL2's 52 and 57 were on the servicing track early in 1956 still wearing their original paint scheme, a gray unit with a blue stripe, but without the original three digit numbers. *(This page)* On Sundays, the F3's always lined up for the "official" EMD pose in front of the BAR water tank. With light traffic on that day, most sets would come to Northern Maine Jct. for washing and servicing to be prepared for the next week's assignments. The EMD cab unit noses were always very colorful when lined up together. The BAR color scheme, added to this nose, was most attractive and photographed beautifully.

(Above) It was a summer like day in May of 1957 when F3 #47 brought #2 the AROOSTOOK FLYER to a stop at the Northern Maine Jct. passenger shed, the last stop before Bangor. Two of the F3's, #46 and 47, were equipped with steam generators for passenger service. The BAR tried to attract passengers with modern equipment but in the end lost to the automobile. *(Below)* Yard switching power for the BAR changed during the 50's from NW2's to ex New Haven GE-Cooper Bessemer Y's. #33 and #34 still retained their New Haven green paint in May 1957 while working at Northern Maine Jct. #30 was painted into full BAR colors and was regularly assigned to Northern Maine Jct. With double reduction gearing for maximum traction, these units could move anything in the yard but not above a speed of 25mph.

(Above) #44-43-45 were all lined up elephant style in storage awaiting their call for the fall potato rush. Just out of overhaul, the units were in excellent condition, showing off their beautiful F3 lines. They were Phase II units with "chicken wire" covering the openings between the portholes. The B units had already been sold to the PRR when this photograph was taken in September of 1958. *(Below)* #50 was the first of eight BL2's delivered to the BAR. Rotated past E7 #11, the unit stopped for a pose under the distinctive water tower at the diesel shop. BL2's lasted into the mid 80's on the BAR, a credit to the shop forces at Northern Maine Jct. Just like the F3's, the BL2's received a complete overhaul on a regularly scheduled basis.

(Above) #78 switched a cut over the MEC headed toward the Searsport connection. It was hard to miss those red-white & blue box cars kept so clean by the BAR as traveling advertisements for the State of Maine. #78 was one of only six GP9's on the system and a member of the team that went to work for the PRR. It was handling potatoes in Maine during the winter and iron ore in Ohio during the summer. These units were delivered from EMD with two digit numbers in June of 1954. *(Below)* Because of the BL2's and later GP7's, the BAR did not acquire many switch engines. Four NW2's handled all the assignments until the arrival of the second hand Y's from the New Haven. In the early years, these units handled some branch line duties later assigned to road switchers. Delivered with the BL2's, these units continued the dieselization process on the BAR. #23 was photographed at Northern Maine Jct. in October 1959. Originally numbered #800 to 803, all four NW2's had been sold to other short lines by 1970.

(Above) In September of 1956, F3 #671 led the MEC's through freight south to Rigby yard in South Portland. Made up in Bangor, the train would stop at Northern Maine Jct. for a BAR pick up. Just the same as the BAR's F3's, these were Phase II units with "chicken wire" over the openings. Two A units and two B units were delivered in December 1947 with steam generators in the B's for possible passenger service. The photography day was a beautiful fall one with very distinctive clouds in the sky. *(Below)* On the next day, the same train had a different set of power. Leading was #565, a freight GP7 with dynamic brakes, and one of the two RS11's. Trailing the consist was a red passenger GP7 without dynamic braking. Waiting for the freight to clear was the section foreman and his reliable "putt-putt."

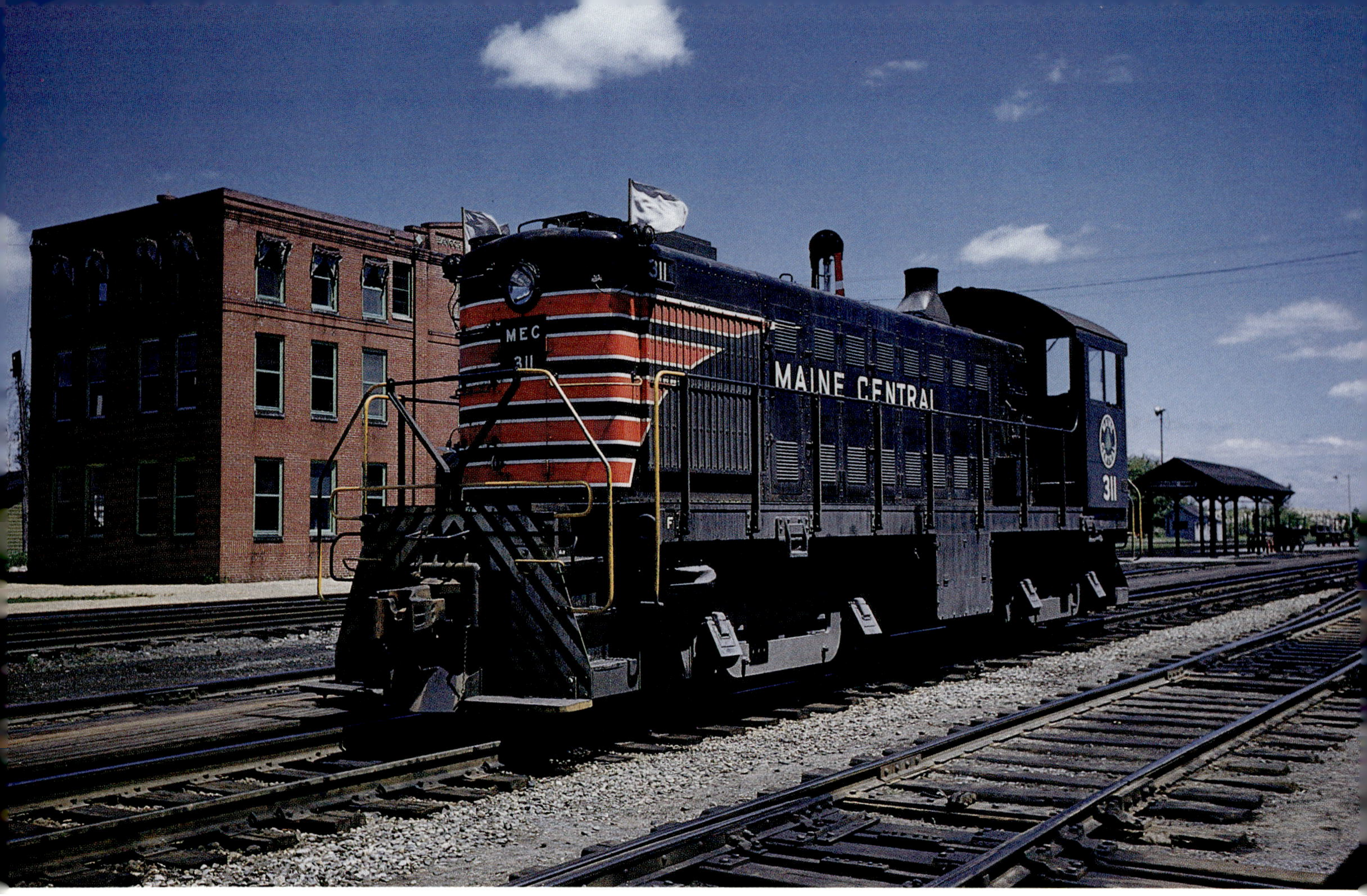
MEC
311
MAINE CENTRAL
311

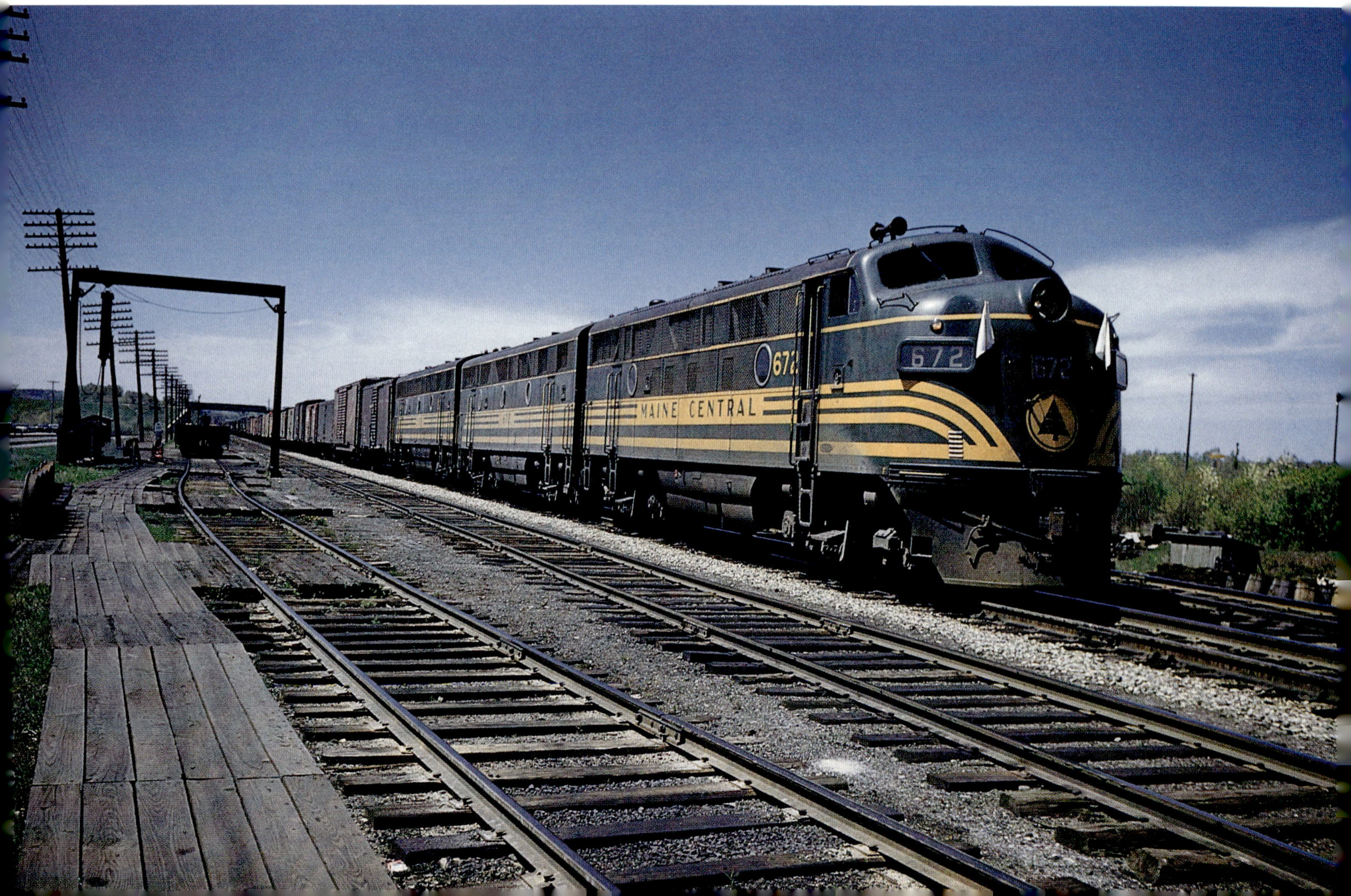
672
MAINE CENTRAL

(Opposite page, top) Sometimes the MEC local would stop to set off or pick up cars. S4 #311 stopped to pick up weigh-bills from the BAR office, its white flags clearly visible, representing an "extra" - an unscheduled train. #311 was one of the two S4's delivered in the black switcher scheme and equipped with MU only on the cab end. Later S4 units were delivered in green indicating a road switcher and were equipped with MU on both ends. But #311's biggest distinction was being the first production S4 built in the United States. MEC #311 and 312 were built as a joint order with B&M S4's #1266-#1273 when the two railroads were under joint control.

(Opposite page, bottom) #672 with the only two MEC F3 B units arrived from Portland with a set off for the BAR. In May of 1957, it was hard to find complete sets in green during the transition years when the MEC was changing from red to green. The striping on the B units did not go the complete way across the carbody, but was rounded off on the #2 end. During 1966, all the F3's were traded in on GP38's.

(This page, above) About to pass under the BAR bridge was a four unit consist, an F3 and an F5 bracketing the two RS11's. Tonnage was heavier in February 1959 requiring the extra unit on the southbound. Whenever possible, the Maine Central led with a cab unit to insure the best visibility for the crew. Lots of potatoes were moving out of the warehouses south, down the eastern coast to Boston, New York, and Washington.

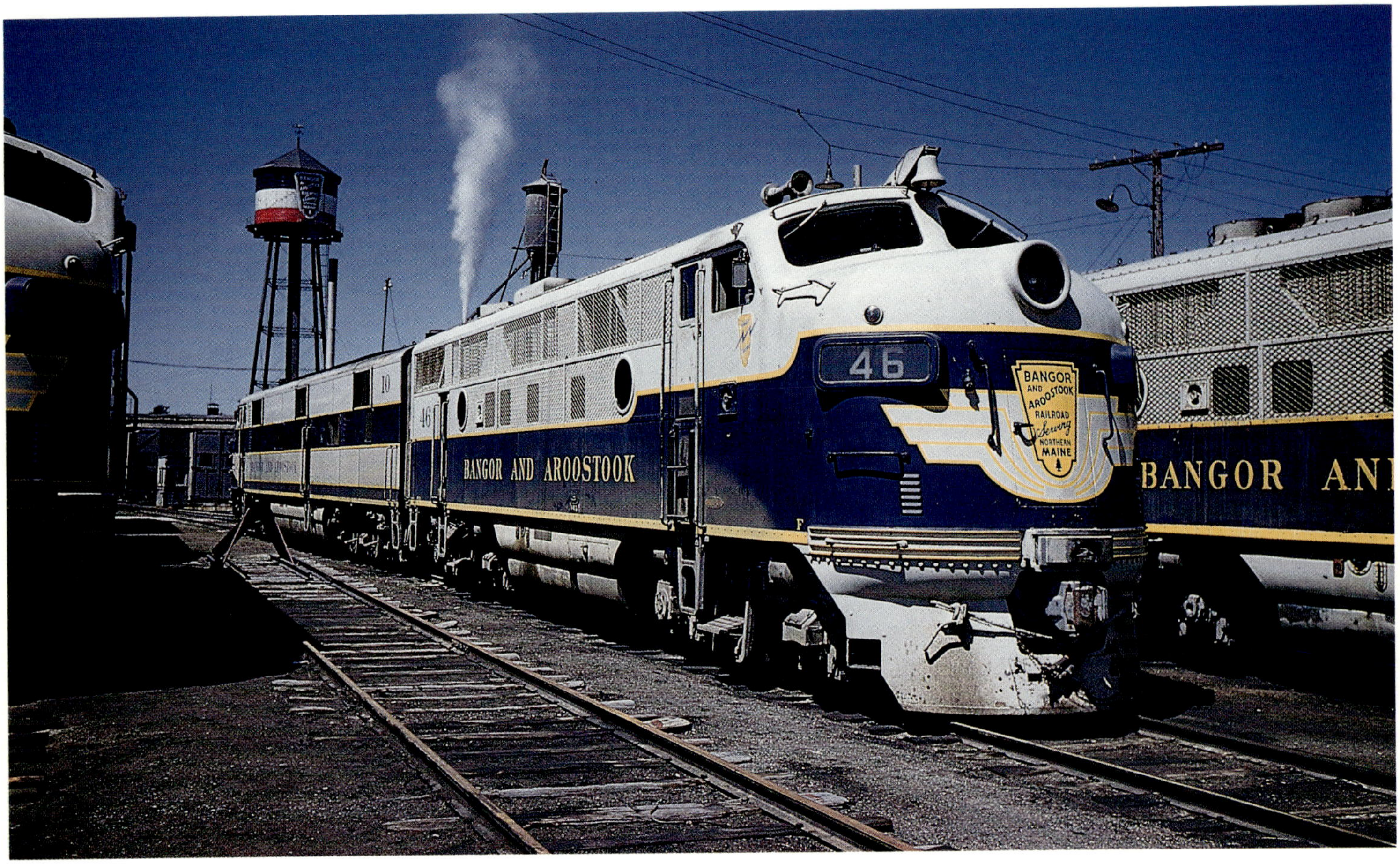

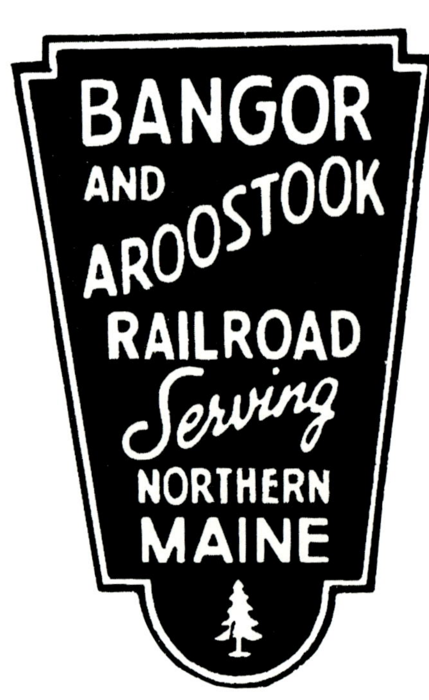

(Above) On May 5, 1957 steam generator equipped F3 #46 idled with an E7 at Northern Maine Junction engine terminal. BAR received two F3 A-B-A sets in 1947 and two more in 1948, however the B units were later sold to the PRR. #46 & 47 were used extensively through the years in passenger service. Because of problems in heavy packed snow and frozen air lines, the BAR moved the bell to a bracket over the cab. At least two of these F3's have been saved for future generations to see.

(Opposite page, top) BL2 #54 was being serviced in May of 1957 as a single unit. #54 had been repainted, but for some unknown reason not relettered Bangor and Aroostook. Most of the time in road service the BL2's were used as trailing units behind cab units for better visibility of the engineer. The BL2 was a strange combination of cab unit and roadswitcher. Even with its limitations, the BAR made the most of this branchline unit. With only 59 units in production, the BL was not a common sight on most carriers except for the BAR. The BL2's were delivered as #550 to #557 but were renumbered in 1953 to #50-#57.

(Opposite page, bottom) Occasionally the B&M's only E8 would make an appearance at Northern Maine Jct. In conjunction with a Maine Central E7, B&M #3821 was only six miles from its final destination, Bangor station, in October of 1959. Within two years this unit was retired and later sold to Mo Pac as their #42. The E8 came on the scene just a little too late to make the MEC or BAR rosters. By 1950, most of the New England roads had obtained their EMD passenger units in the form of E7's. #3821 was joined in New England by other E8's from the CP and NYC.

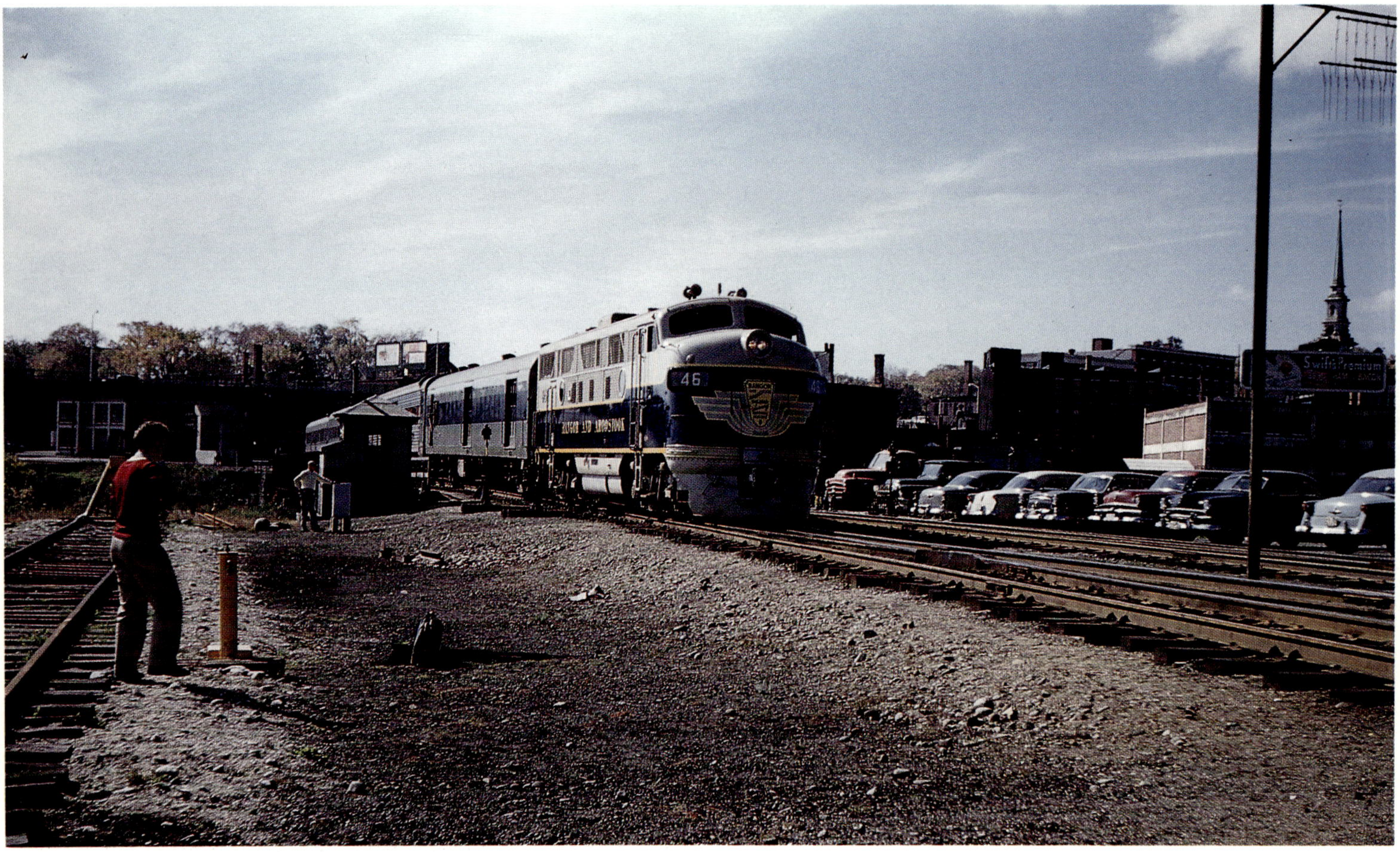

Bangor, Me.

Bangor Maine is the second largest city in the state. It is about 135 miles northeast of Portland and 60 miles up the Penobscot River from the Atlantic Ocean. By 1800, Bangor was a growing port for the export of lumber. In 1836, one of the first railroads in Maine built a 12 mile line along the Penobscot River from Old Town to Bangor to bring lumber to the docks.

(Above) #46 arrived at Bangor station with the AROOSTOOK FLYER in September 1955. The switch tender watched the four car consist as the train passed into the train shed. The first car was a Pullman Standard "American Flyer" lightweight RPO-Baggage, unique to the BAR. #46 was one of the two F3's equipped with steam generators used for passenger service.

(Opposite page, top) After making the BAR connection, B&M #3818 departed with the MEC/B&M train for Boston with plenty of head end business. Bangor must have been a "Ford" town with the line up at the station. The Boston & Maine purchased E7's in four groups between 1945 and 1949. #3818 was one of the four, #3816-#3819, purchased in 1948. #3820 came in April 1949 during the last month of production; however, not many color photographs exist of #3820 as she was wrecked at Nashua, N.H. in November of 1954 and then scrapped.

(Opposite page, bottom) Switching by the old train shed was #301, one of the three 1949 S2's on the Maine Central. The scene was captured in 1955 and the MEC was still doing a good passenger business on the through trains to Portland and Boston. Most New England roads purchased some S2's for their switching duties. With good care from the Bangor enginehouse, the units lasted right into the late 1970's, some with over thirty years of service. The MEC S2's were numbered #301-303.

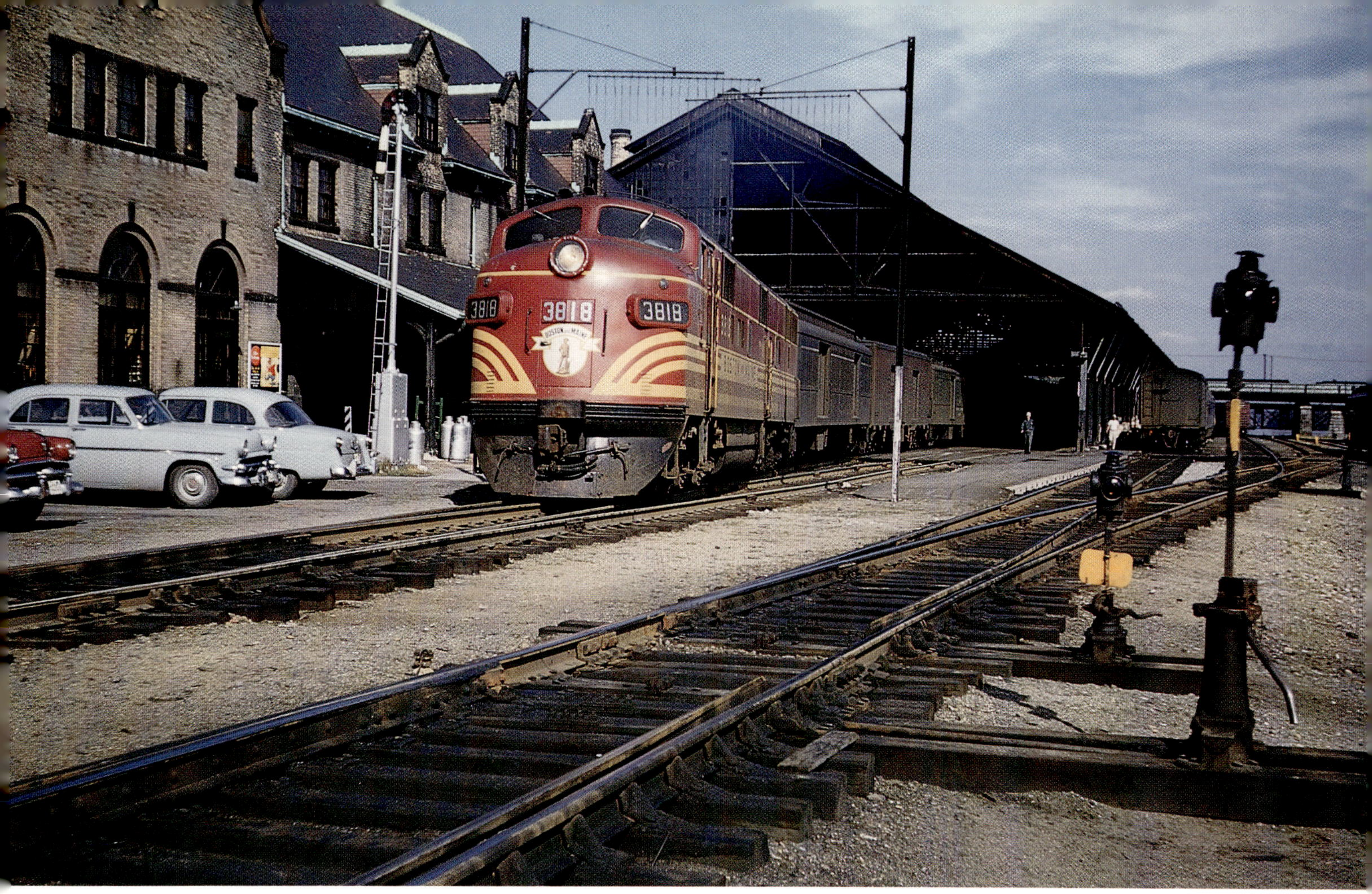
3818
3818
3818

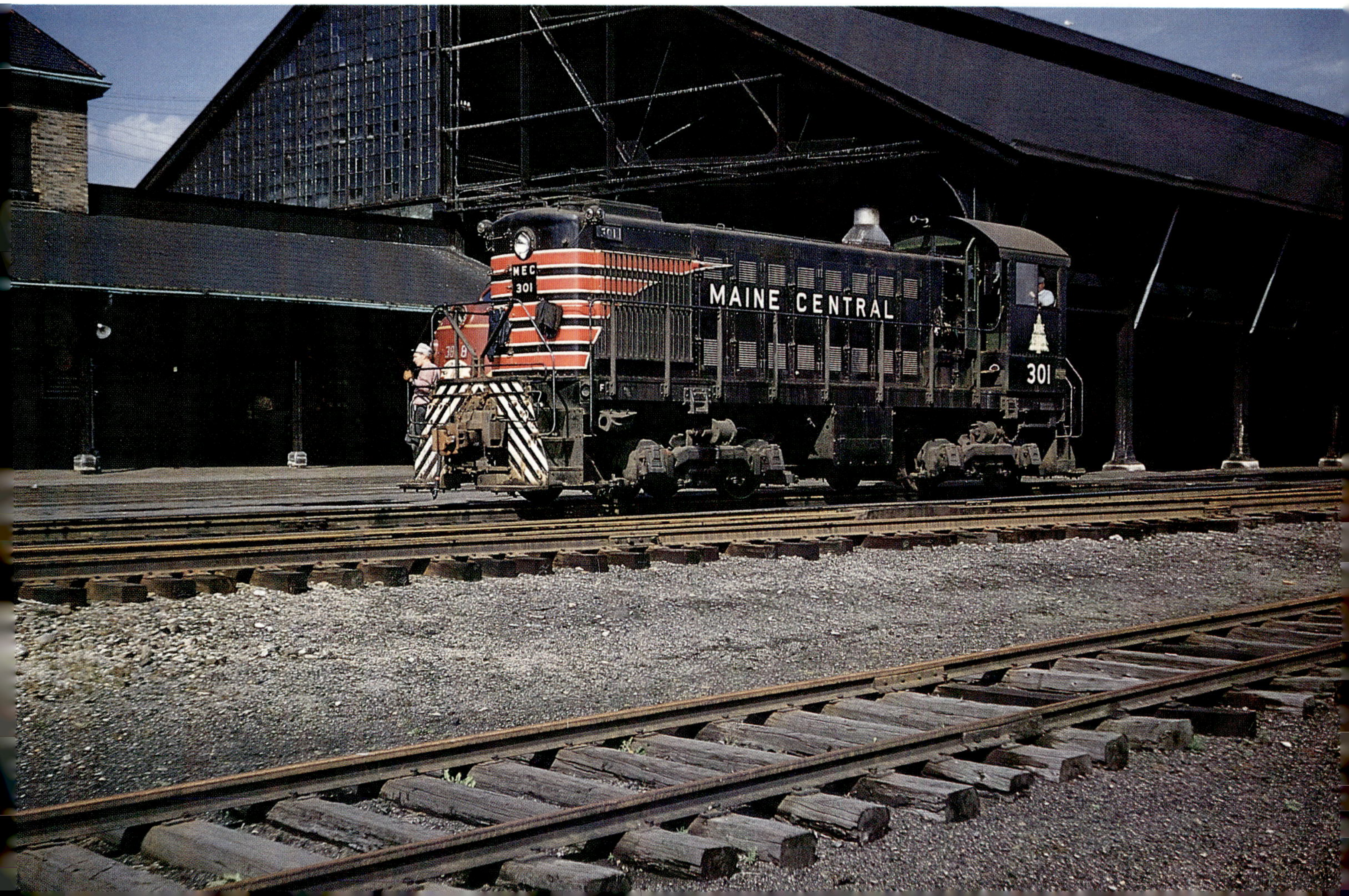
MAINE CENTRAL
301
MEC
301

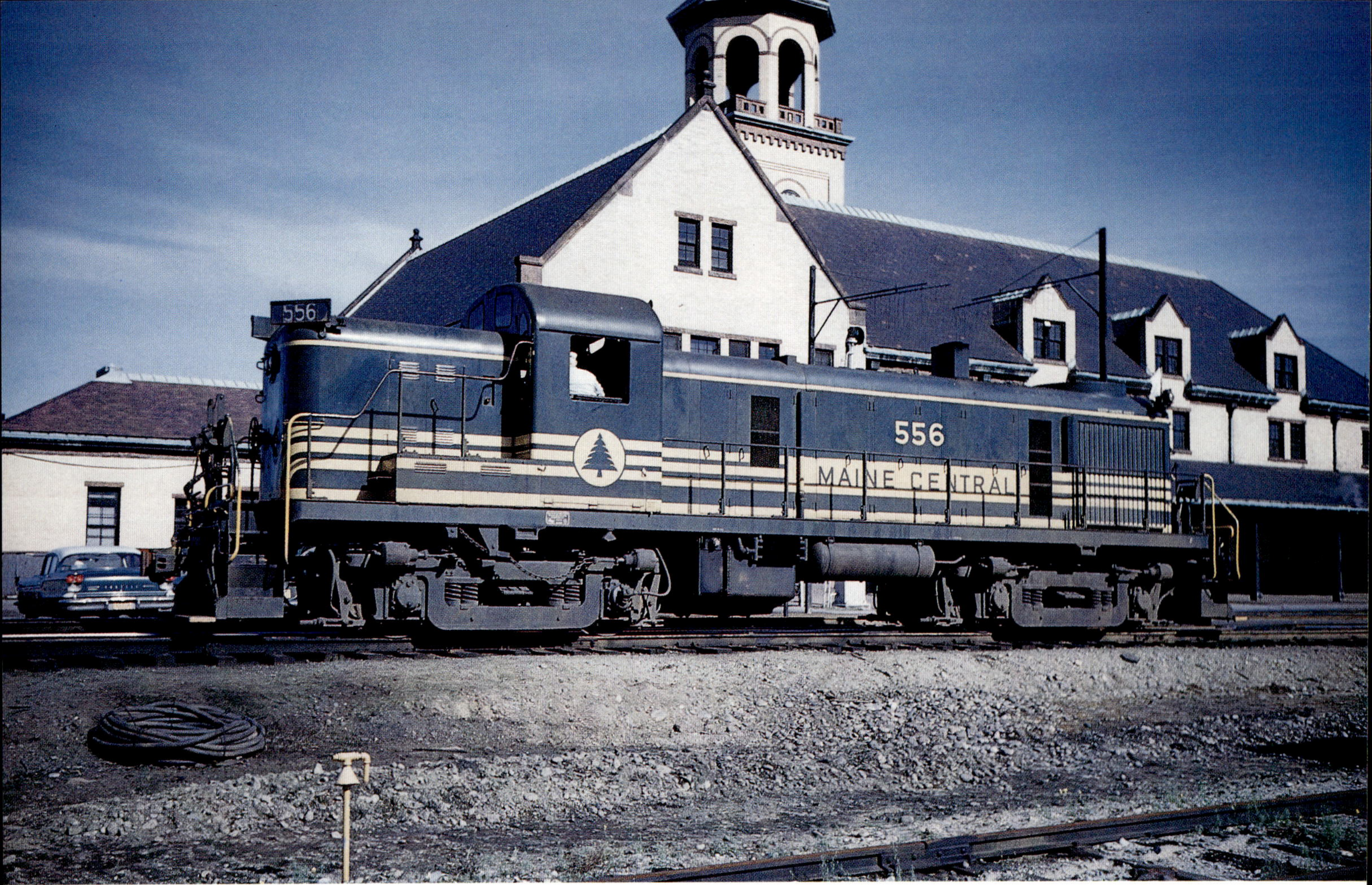

556
MAINE CENTRAL
556

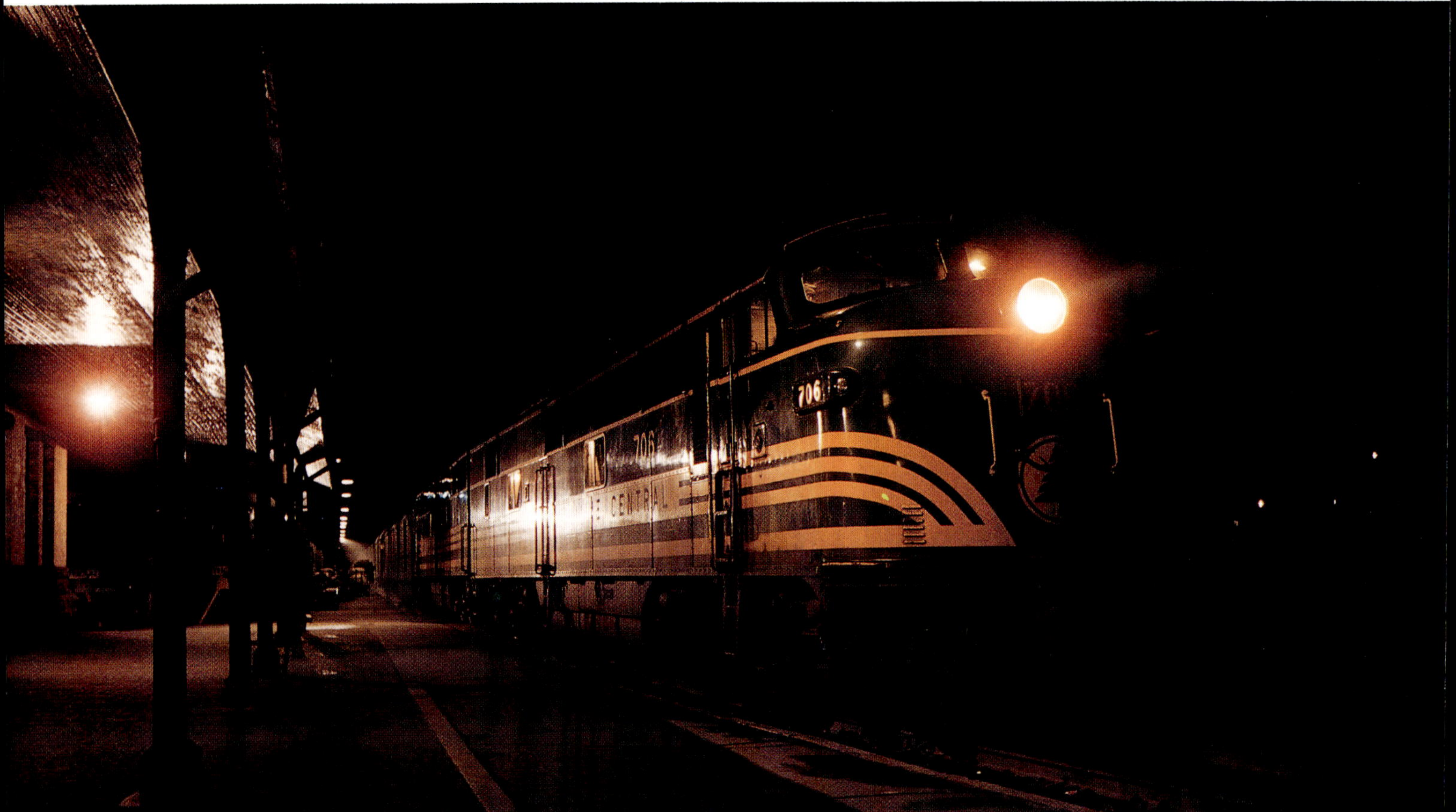

706
CENTRAL

(Above) Also on the Maine Central's 1949 order list to Alco, were five RS2's, the first road switchers on the system. As steam was being phased out, Bangor became an Alco city with S1's, S2's, S4's, RS2's, RS3's and RS11's being maintained there. Many of the RS2's wore a modified green paint scheme. In October of 1958, #552 and #554 joined together for a trip north to Vanceboro, Maine near the Canadian border. Maine Central's group of RS2's were numbered #551 to #555.

(Opposite page, top) Silhouetted against the Bangor Union Station in October of 1958, idled MEC #556. Built five years before this photograph, this Phase III RS3 had the typical identifying features of 45 degree number boards and two vertical filter openings on the long hood. Maine Central made the RS3 owners' list with two units, #556 and #557. Over the years, Bangor, Maine became the home base for these units. That beautiful light brick station was torn down signalling the end of passenger service.

(Opposite page, bottom) Every night, the overnight train the GULL from St. John passed through Bangor station on its way to Boston. Loaded with Pullman sleepers, coaches and head end business, the train usually commanded two E7's. E7 #706 cools its traction motors during the station stop on this May evening in 1959 beside the Penobscot River. #706 would finish her career working for the Kansas City Southern as #7 in a warmer climate.

(Above) By the 1870's the European and North American Railroad had completed a route from Bangor to New Brunswick. At Old Town, Maine north of Bangor, three RS3's and RS2's had their train rolling at 40mph, a train load of box cars for Vanceboro, Maine and the CP connection. The date was November 11, 1956 and a touch of snow was already on the ground. This was the "Alco" line of the Maine Central.

(Opposite page, top) The second freight cab unit on the system was #672, an F3 A unit. The turntable operator helped the hostler center the unit at the balance point before rotation. It was now January 1957, the weather was much colder and ice built up on the sides of the cab units formed by run off of snow from the warmer car body roof. In the background was one of the BAR E7's being serviced after the AROOSTOOK FLYER passenger run. #671 A&B and #672 A&B were Maine Central's group of four Phase II F3's built by EMD in December of 1947.

(Opposite page, bottom) Like most of the New England roads, Maine Central was also a member of the 44 tonner club. In October of 1958, #15 was stationed at Bangor. Seven units were purchased from 1941 through 1947 to cover light switching assignments. Fortunately for #15, the unit was sold in December of 1974 to the Conway Scenic Railroad at North Conway, N.H. and has been maintained there in excellent condition.

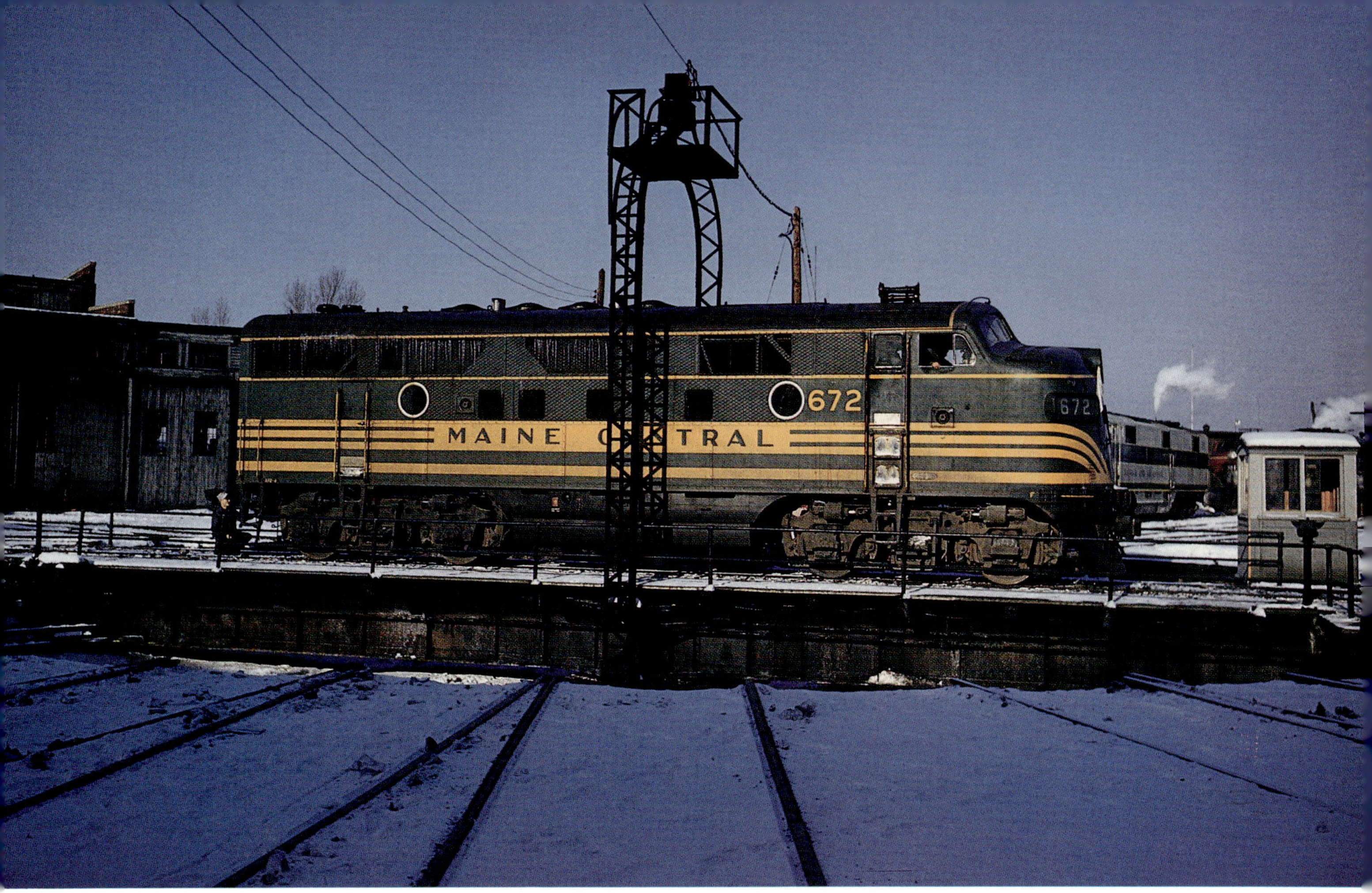
672
MAINE
672

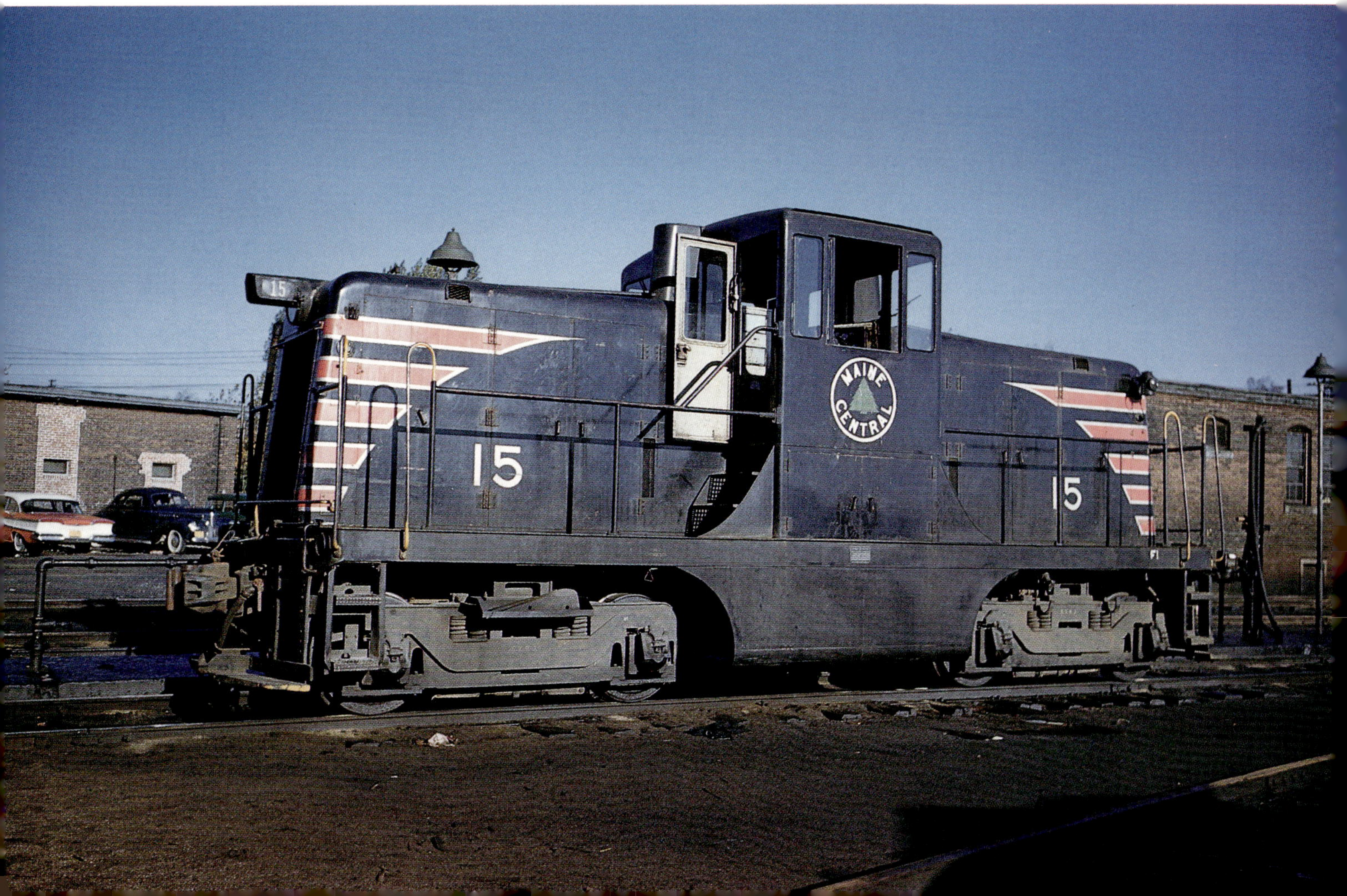
15
MAINE CENTRAL
15
15

BANGOR
AROOSTOOK
RAILROAD
NORTHERN
MAINE
10
BANGOR AND AROOSTOOK
10

3811
BOSTON and MAINE
3811
BOSTON and MAINE

(Below) At the very end of F3 production, Maine Central received six A units #681-686 in November 1948. These transition units between F3's and F7's were sometimes known as F5's. While being serviced at Bangor in May of 1959, #685 was prepared to be the lead unit for the southbound consist. #685 would remain in green until traded in to EMD seven years later. From a low angle, this unit looked like an F7; however, it was built three months before F7 production.

Bangor was known as the E7 capital of Northern New England by railfans. Passenger trains with E7's from the BAR, B&M, and MEC arrived and departed daily from the MEC station. Displaying blue, red, and green color schemes, these units would "head for the barn" for servicing at the MEC enginehouse. Four hundred and twenty-nine E7 A units were built from 1945 to 1949 with thirty units seeing Bangor from time to time. BAR #701 and #702, later #10 and #11, were delivered in April 1949. *(Opposite page, top)* In January 1957, #10 had just arrived off the AROOSTOOK FLYER for servicing. The steam generator was popping off through the roof vent. Behind this BAR E7 *(opposite page, bottom)* was B&M #3811, part of the second group of B&M E7's. Even without a train, the steam generator on E units had to run to produce steam for the cab heaters. The steam exhaust under the cab indicated the cab heaters were working just fine.

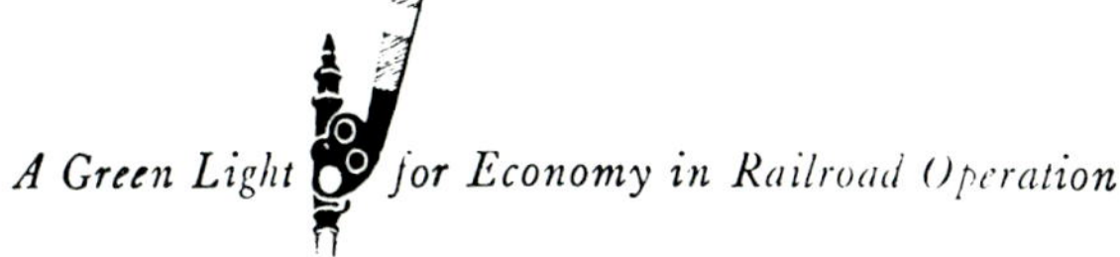

Greenville, Me.

For a shorter more direct route from Montreal to Saint John, New Brunswick, the Canadian Pacific needed a route across northern Maine. In 1885, the CP International Railway of Maine built a railroad across to Mattawamkeag where it could connect with the European and North American Railroad to Vanceboro. Completed in 1889, the line formed a major artery to Halifax using joint trackage with Maine Central from Mattawamkeag to Vanceboro. Greenville, on the southern tip of Moosehead Lake, was located on the CP line. In 1884 the BAR also entered Greenville from the south and established an interchange, mainly for car loads of wood pulp.

As winter approached the sleepy International of Maine came alive with traffic diverted from the frozen St. Lawrence River for export to Europe. *(Above)* On a very overcast and cold Maine winter day, #4027 plus two RS3's and another FA led a general merchandise train westward toward Megantic, Quebec. #4027 was the last FA-1 built by MLW for the CP. Because it was the last FA-1, #4027 carried the vertical slat grille usually found on the FA-2's. In January 1958, Greenville had a lot of snow on the ground around the station. The interchange track leading to the right led to the BAR yard.

(Opposite page, top) At the BAR, BL2 #56 switched out several loads of wood pulp for the CP connection before returning to Derby. During these below zero days, bay windows were a necessity for the engineer while switching, but it didn't afford any protection for the ground man. Winter railroading in Maine was a tough job.

(Opposite page, bottom) One year later in January 1959, it was a clear day, but now 20 degrees below zero with a strong north wind off the frozen lake. One year old RS18 #8764 led a nine year old FB-1 on a westbound freight. With that extreme temperature, one did not stay outside long with a camera or move far from the warmth of the station.

BANGOR & AROOSTOOK
56
56

8764
8764
CANADIAN PACIFIC
CANADIAN PACIFIC

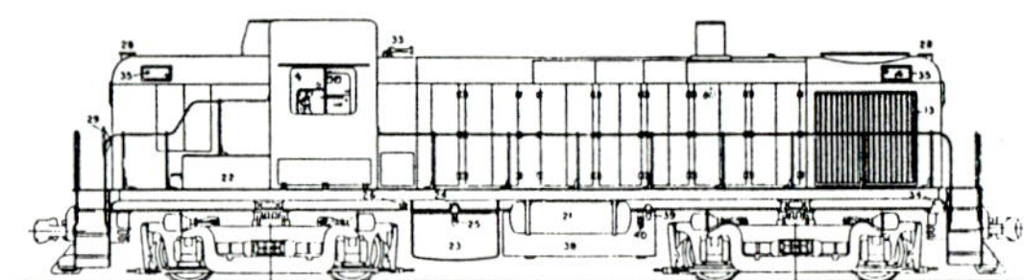

(Above) With the westbound having superiority, the eastbound led by #8434 pulled out of the siding after #8764 cleared. The three 244 diesel engines worked up through the notches, after all the slack was out, and the "van," caboose in CP terms, was moving. As the three unit set moved onto the main, frozen Moosehead Lake was clearly visible. Another notch on the throttle caused some more smoke as the turbos tried to get up to speed. Perfect time for a shot.

(Opposite page, top) The set was now moving at 15mph when the trailing units passed the heated water tank. The stacks were now clear as the 244 engine turbos were up to speed each producing their full 1500/1600hp. With a cab roof number board, the trailing FA-1 #4001 was the second CP cab unit and an Alco built unit. #4409, the middle B unit, was built by MLW in Montreal.

(Opposite page, bottom) During a return trip to Greenville in April 1966, the weather was milder and most of the snow melted. Traffic was still heavy with the St. Lawrence frozen over. Most of the Alco/MLW cab units been traded in on newer power, but this was still very much an Alco product territory for the CP. At track speed, a four unit consist moved past the Greenville station platform. An RS18 led two RS10's and an RS3, with the second unit #8542 painted in the new script lettering.

4001
CANADIAN PACIFIC 4001
4409 CANADIAN PACIFIC

8735
CANADIAN PACIFIC 8735
8592

RAILROAD CROSSING
41
BANGOR AND AROOSTOOK
RAILROAD CROSSING
STOP ON RED SIGNAL

62
NG DEPT S
62
BANGOR AND AROOSTOOK

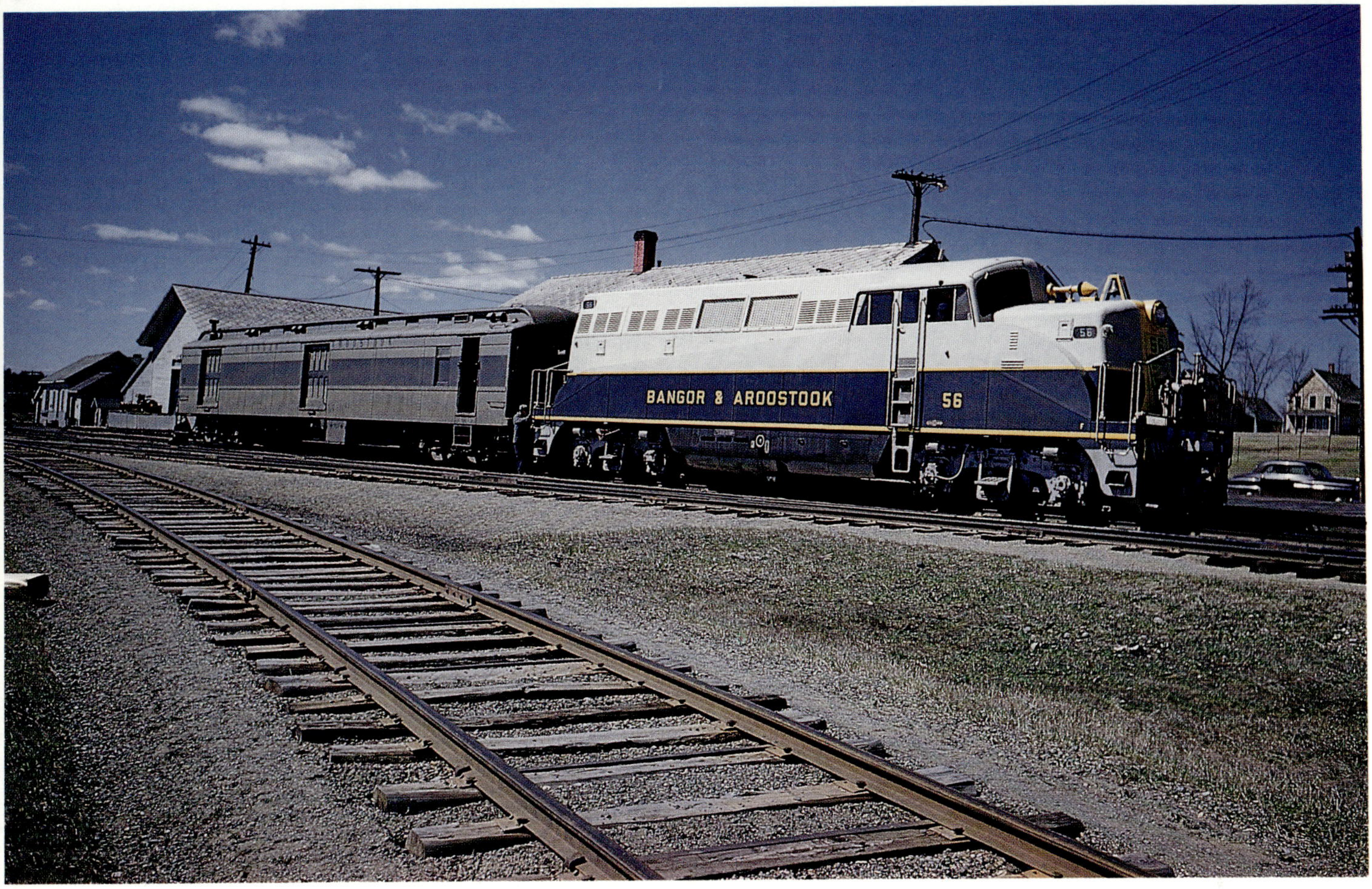

Derby, Milo, and Millinocket, Me.

(Above) At the other end of the Greenville line was Derby, the connection with the BAR mainline. Daily except Sunday, mixed train #9 ran 48.8 miles from Derby to Greenville and returned as train #12. The trestle at Bunker Brook restricted the use of most units for this branch. BL2's #51 and #56 were modified by the removal of counter-weights and limited to 400 gallons of fuel to make this run. At 10:45am, #56 completed her round trip, dropping three loads of wood pulp in the yard before bringing the baggage car to the station. This was a mixed train, however there was limited capacity for passengers in the baggage car. The date was May 4, 1957.

(Opposite page, top) Just north of Milo, Maine, #41 led #10 and #43 on a southbound freight in October 1962, an F3-E7-F3 set. F3's #41 and #43 were no strangers to freight service, but #10 had ended her passenger service the year before in 1961. Modified with a 62:15 freight gear ratio and 38 inch wheels, E7 #10 started a new career in freight service. Within six years, all three units were traded in on new GP38's.

(Opposite page, bottom) Earlier the same day, #62, the third GP7 on the roster, switched some very old camp cars at Millinocket, Maine. The BAR final-ly rostered 16 GP7's, the largest diesel group on the system. By 1962, most of the Geeps were now in the dark blue color scheme, some with large numbers, but others like #62 in small numbers. Originally numbered #560 to #575, the GP7's were renum-bered #60 to #75 in 1953.

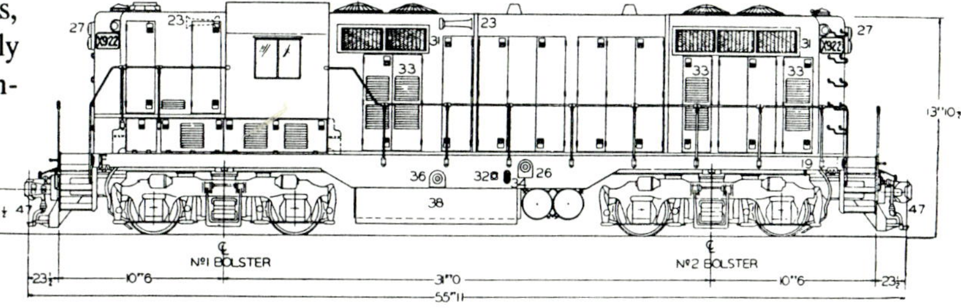

Brownville Jct., Me.

Brownville Jct. was a division point on the International of Maine Division of the Canadian Pacific. It was a railroad town and a junction with the BAR. Even the basketball team was known as the "Railroaders." Because the line was built to high standards, all of the modern classes of steam power could operate on the line including the two 4-8-4's. *(This page)* In November of 1957, #5454 slowly made its way across the bridge and into Brownville Jct. yard. Leaning out the cab window, the fireman watched carefully to make sure that the route had been properly lined for the big 2-8-2. #5454 was a P-2-j Mikado built by Montreal Locomotive Works in 1944, one of the newer 2-8-2's on the line. Between 1940 and 1948 the Canadian Pacific acquired a group of 57 semi-streamlined Mikados #5405-5461.

(Opposite page) US constructed steam locomotives, built to Canadian Pacific specifications, handled most of the yard, local and work train assignments on the International of Maine, because most of the runs were in the United States. *(Top)* #3529, a 1907 Baldwin product, was awaiting her 2nd trick switching assignment at Brownville Jct. yard in October 1958. During the mid fifties #3519 and #3529 were assigned to this I of M division along with two Alco D-10-k 4-6-0's and G2 4-6-2's. It was a small USA steam group within the huge Canadian Pacific roster assigned to the CP operation in the US. With the Vermont operations converted to diesel in 1949, the I of M kept steam into the late 1950's. *(Center and bottom)* That very distinctive Canadian Pacific D-10-k ten wheeler #1082 assigned to Brownville Jct. had just finished her run on the "Scoot." The builders plate read American Locomotive Company, Schenectady Works, October 1912, one of the last two ten wheelers to operate on a class 1 railroad in the US.

(Above) Pacific #2626 arrived with the "Scoot" from Megantic, the last steam powered mixed train in New England. In November 1959, this was pay day for the railroaders and the last car in the train was the "Pay Car." Just as soon as the wheels came to rest, the line formed at the rear. The brick station was a CP standard design serving the "Scoot" during the day and the ATLANTIC LIMITED at night. *(Below)* Just south of Brownville Jct. in May 1957, E7 #10 handled train #2 the AROOSTOOK FLYER. Better know as the "Flyer," this four car train was heading for Bangor from Van Buren, Maine, making the 235 mile run in about six hours. The first and last cars were pre war "American Flyer" lightweight equipment and the center two were Pullman Standard coaches delivered after WWII. The "American Flyer" cars were part of a 1937 seven car order from Pullman Standard for three buffet-lounge cars, two coaches, and two baggage-mail cars.

(Left) During the 1950's, a group of 40' steel box cars were stenciled for the Canadian Pacific International of Maine Division to handle the US loadings. They were a common sight on the mixed train "Scoot" and in the train yard at Brownville Jct.

(Right) Another common item in the "Scoot's" consist was a wooden CP "van." Coupled behind the combine, this wooden caboose was the mobile base for the conductor to handle the waybills along the route. Since this train was a day run in both directions, the crew seldom used the bunks for sleeping quarters. The only modernization was in the form of an electric light, powered from the combine next door. Between Brownville

Jct. and Greenville, there were several small towns, served only by the railroad. The "Scoot" brought in all the supplies and the crew had a close relationship with all the natives that they served. *(Bottom)* Nearly the entire winter Brownville Jct. yard was covered with snow, but as the winter progressed, the snow got deeper. After a heavy snow fall, there were no more places to put it without taking a track or two out of service. A snow crew would be called out to shovel snow onto flats for disposal out over the river bridge. With an old 2-8-0 for motive power, the work train would slowly remove the over abundance of snow to keep the yard in operation.

In January of 1959, the 2-8-0's had been bumped from regular duty by an Alco S2. Built by Alco in 1949, #7097 *(below)* was one of the three originally purchased for the CP Vermont operations. By the long shadows and the amount of snow on the ground, we know it was another long cold Maine winter. At zero the radiator shutter remained closed most of the time but the cab heaters would keep the wooden lining in the cab warm for the crew.

The days are short and the winter long, especially in Brownville Jct., Maine. As the sun sets, an S2 did its final switching chores for the day and we close this book on *New England Rails*. Another time will bring another book on this beautiful area of many railroads.